The Mysterious Case of the Stone of Destiny

A Scottish Historical Detective Whodunnit!

DAVID MAULE

Illustrations by **Rob Hands**

TIPPERMUIR
· BOOKS LIMITED ·

The Mysterious Case of the Stone of Destiny – David Maule
Copyright © 2024. All rights reserved.

The right of David Maule to be identified as the author of the Work has been asserted in accordance with the Copyright, Designs & Patents Act 1988.

This first edition published and copyright 2024 by
Tippermuir Books Ltd, Perth, Scotland.

mail@tippermuirbooks.co.uk – www.tippermuirbooks.co.uk.

No part of this publication may be reproduced or used in any form or by any means without written permission from the Publisher except for review purposes. All rights whatsoever in this book are reserved.

ISBN 978-1-913836-26-9 (paperback).

A CIP catalogue record for this book is available from the British Library.

Project coordination and editorial by Paul S Philippou.

Cover design by Matthew Mackie.

Illustrations and maps: Rob Hands.

Editorial support: Ajay Close, Steve Zajda and Jean Hands.

Co-founders and publishers of Tippermuir Books: Rob Hands, Matthew Mackie and Paul S Philippou.

Text design, layout, and artwork by Bernard Chandler [graffik].
Text set in Times New Roman MT Std 10.5/14pt with Gill Sans Std titling.

Printed and bound by Ashford Colour Press.

'*A Gripping Historical Whodunnit*'
'The fate of the legendary Stone of Destiny, aka the Stone of Scone, remains one of the most abiding mysteries in Scottish history. Intrigue and controversy have surrounded this enigmatic artefact from earliest times to the modern day when this symbol of royal power was taken from Edinburgh to Westminster Abbey for Charles III's coronation. But was that the original stone used to enthrone Scotland's ancient kings, or a substitute? One of the points made in the book is that the original had a different shape.

Meticulously researched, *The Mysterious Case of the Stone of Destiny* reads like a gripping historical whodunnit. David Maule leaves no stone unturned as he casts a forensic eye over the evidence. His fact-finding process – investigating its origins and background, scrutinising the witnesses and identifying possible suspects – comes to some surprising conclusions. Whether or not you agree with his verdict about the Stone of Destiny's final resting place, this incisive and entertaining inquiry is a must-read for those interested in Scottish history and for lovers of historical mysteries.'
Marie Macpherson, author of *The Knox Trilogy*

'*The Mysterious Case of the Stone of Destiny* has been rigorously researched from both primary and secondary sources, yet it is presented in plain language as an objective and even-handed investigation, not unlike a contemporary detective novel, *except that none of the characters are fictional and all of them have been dead for around 700 years.*

David Maule lays the case before us like an impartial advocate, leaving us, the jury, to form our own conclusions. *The Mysterious Case of the Stone of Destiny* is a compelling read - a page-turner - and will be enjoyed by professional historians and lay-readers alike. I loved it!"
Charles MacLean, MBE, author of *Spirit of Place: Whisky Distilleries of Scotland* and *Whiskypedia: An Introduction to Scotch Whisky*.

'If you were to present the Stone of Destiny to a group of skilled stonemasons used to working with historical buildings but who had no background knowledge of this particular piece of rock, and ask them what possible purpose it might have had, the chances are they would assign to it a far lowlier function than it currently enjoys as a central feature of coronations in Britain. I did do this, and the general view seems to be that the stone most likely slotted into an ancient church or perhaps castle floor and concealed something important below – an access to a secret tunnel, perhaps, or to a hiding place for objects of value. Those same skilled masons still work in the traditions followed by their artisan ancestors in Norman cathedrals over a thousand years ago, and the same pride that drives the renovation of those impossibly heavy but apparently weightless structures today was no doubt present amongst those who crafted the original lofty buildings. So it's hard to believe that a partly-dressed stone with such crude hacking marks should possess such spiritual and historical significance when it has sat for at least a thousand years in surroundings that themselves display the pinnacle of achievements of stonemasonry beauty. That's why I approached David Maule's book with a genuine desire to explore the 'Mysterious Case' of the title.

It is a fascinating book, all the better for its conciseness and clarity of focus. I feel as if I've been part of a conversation in a pub – a good pub, though, where you get proper conversation, and into which has stepped a person with an unusual grasp of historical detail. He quietly introduces a contentious issue then somehow manages to stand back on the edge of the debate and listen. And every time someone raises a question or expresses an opinion, he is on hand to fill in what is known in the historical record. As the book proceeds it becomes more of an interactive experience as the author appeals to our common understanding of human behaviour to share his judgement of the probable allegiances, motives, preferences and prejudices of the assembled cast as he whittles down the suspects to their core. Convincing and entertaining. I should add, though, that I've seen people thrown out of pubs for less.'
Andy Hopkins, Stone carver and sculptor.

The Mysterious Case of the Stone of Destiny

The relics, charters, privileges and other muniments which touch on the royal dignity and the realm of Scotland are to be placed under secure guard inside the realm of Scotland, and under the seals of the greatest of the realm...

Treaty of Birgham, 18 July 1290.

*To my wife, Zeynep, for her encouragement,
support and understanding.*

About the Author

David Maule has had a career in English language teaching, working in Sierra Leone, Turkey and Bosnia then Stevenson College, later Edinburgh College. During this time he wrote a number of coursebooks and readers for learners of English together with papers for the SQA ESOL exams. For twelve years he was editor of the *About Language* section of *Modern English Teacher* magazine.

While working for Stevenson and Edinburgh Colleges, and on occasion for private language schools, together with the British Council Summer School at Stirling University, he gave talks and held classes on various aspects of Scottish history and culture to learners and teachers of English. He also conducted visits to places of interest.

David lives in Edinburgh with his wife, Zeynep. They have two grown-up sons and currently share their house with a golden retriever and two cats.

Acknowledgements

This book has been a long time in gestation and a much earlier version received great encouragement from Charles MacLean, now the author of numerous books about Scotch whisky, at that time working as a literary agent. However, times were different then and despite his efforts the manuscript was unable to find a publisher. Recent events made me determined to revise and update the text and Charles was again very positive and helpful.

I would also like to thank Paul Philippou of Tippermuir Books for adopting the text, and also for editing it. I have worked with a number of editors over the years and it is a testament to Paul's skill and attention to detail that he is the first one I haven't argued with. Thanks too go to Alan Montgomery for reading a later draft of the book and making valuable comments. And to Roben Antoniewicz for the back cover photograph.

A warm thanks also goes to Rob Hands who provided the illustrations for this book and to Matthew Mackie who designed the cover.

Marie MacPherson and I worked in the same language school some years ago and I have followed her career as an author of Scottish history novels with interest. She was kind enough to read the manuscript and make a number of useful points, for which many thanks.

I'd also like to thank the bronze sculptor Michael Snowden, RSA, for his perceptive views on the bronze chair which is discussed in Prosecution I, and the art historian Linda Reynolds for her analysis of the miniature of David I and Malcolm IV in Prosecution II.

Finally, I'd like to thank my wife, Zeynep, to whom this book is dedicated. Having come to Scotland from her native Turkey, and being party to numerous discussions about the manuscript, she probably knows more about this period of Scottish history than she ever needed to know.

After a career in publishing, Andy Hopkins trained in stonemasonry and sculpture. His technical expertise is apparent in the discussion he has contributed, for which I'm very grateful.

The Allegation

That in the summer of 1296, person or persons unknown appropriated the enthronement stone resting in Scone Abbey and that consequently the stone later taken by Edward I of England was a substitute.

Contents

Background I: *March 1286 to September 1296* .. 1

Prosecution I: *Circumstantial Evidence* 4

Prosecution II: *Eyewitness Evidence* 14

Prosecution III: *Eyewitness Testimony* 22

Background II: *July 1298 to June 1314* 35

Defence I: *John Walwayn's Testimony* 37

Defence II: *Lord Hailes' Testimony* 50

The Investigation 61

The Heist 79

The Knowledge 88

Notes are at the end of each chapter.

Preface

In the year 843, Kenneth MacAlpin became the first man to rule over the Picts and the Scots, over what was known as Alba, or Scotland north of the Forth. He wasn't crowned but rather enthroned at the old Pictish capital of Scone.

According to legend, MacAlpin used his own stone for the occasion, having moved it eastwards from Dunstaffnage, in Argyll. Other legends trace his enthronement stone further back, to Iona, to Tara in Ireland, to Spain and to points east. Jacob used it as a pillow some say, and so did St Columba according to others. Legends have attached themselves to this stone like barnacles to a boat and, like barnacles, there tends to be little of substance beneath the shell.

By the time the records had begun to catch up with oral sources, the stone had disappeared, taken south by Edward I of England in the wake of his first invasion of Scotland in 1296. There is, however, another view, one which still breaks the surface from time to time, that Edward got the wrong stone, that someone made a switch and sent him south with a piece of local sandstone.

This book is an examination of that possibility.

David Maule

BACKGROUND I
March 1286 to September 1296

AT THE SIDE OF THE ROAD between Burntisland and Kinghorn, on the coast of Fife, there is a simple monument. It stands on a steep slope above the sea. On that shore, on a morning in March 1286, the king of Scots, Alexander III was found dead, his neck broken. There had been a gale the previous night, from the north and heavy with snow. Alexander was keen to get to Kinghorn, to his new wife, Yolande. He was rowed across the stormy Firth of Forth. Then, riding through the storm he became separated from his companions. That was the last time he was seen alive.

Alexander's death was only the latest in a series which afflicted his family. His sons had died, as had his daughter, the wife of Eric II of Norway. The direct line survived only in her child, the infant Margaret. Known as the Maid of Norway, this child had become heir to the Scottish throne. However, Alexander's widowed queen was rumoured to be carrying his child. The baby, whether boy or girl, would have a better claim to succeed than the Maid. There was nothing to do except wait for results.

In this febrile atmosphere the voices of other claimants began to be heard. The aged Bruce of Annandale and John Balliol, both descendants of David I, exchanged strong words at the Scone parliament of 1286. At that meeting six Guardians were appointed. By the end of the year it was clear that the queen's pregnancy had come to nothing and that winter there was fighting in the south-west between Robert the Bruce and John Balliol. The Guardians re-established control and the kingdom settled down to a precarious peace.

Negotiations followed with England and Norway resulting in a marriage agreement known as the Treaty of Birgham. It paired up the Maid with the young heir to the English crown, Edward of Caernarfon. This was not a treaty of union. It clearly stated that Scotland should be separate and divided from England, free in itself and without subjection. The way was now clear for Margaret to take the Scottish throne. She did not, however, survive the crossing, dying in Orkney. Both Bruce and Balliol now saw themselves as the next in line and the country prepared itself for civil war.

Against this threatening background Bishop Fraser of St Andrews wrote to Edward I of England to ask for his intervention. The following June Edward presided over the court called to assess the claims of Balliol and Bruce and eleven others who saw themselves as the next king of Scots. In November 1292 judgement was pronounced in favour of Balliol. He was enthroned at Scone on 30 November, St Andrew's Day.

Looked on by his subjects as king and by Edward as a vassal, his position was rather complex. For three years he walked the narrow tightrope between war and total humiliation. In 1295 the balancing act came to an end. Edward was at war with France. In October the Scots drafted an offensive and defensive alliance with the French.

A force led by the earl of Buchan drove into Cumberland and attacked Carlisle. Towards the end of the month Edward crossed the Tweed and took Berwick. A considerable part of the population was massacred. On 27 April the two armies met near Dunbar. The Scots scattered before the English attack. Edinburgh Castle surrendered after five days. At Stirling Castle only the porter stayed to hand over the keys. Edward began what amounted to a royal progress through northern Scotland, collecting fealties as he went, though most of these were recorded in Berwick in August. The final document became known as the Ragman Roll, possibly due to the number of seals attached.

King John met him near Montrose and confessed his rebellion. Later he renounced the French treaty and was ceremonially stripped of his kingdom, a degrading process which involved all the symbols of royalty, from the crown on his head to the costly fur on his tabard, being taken from him. He emerged as Toom Tabard, the empty jacket.

On his way south Edward stopped over in Perth and at this time a stone was removed from nearby Scone Abbey and sent to Westminster.

PROSECUTION I: CIRCUMSTANTIAL EVIDENCE

John Balliol with his crown and sceptre broken and tabard torn.

PROSECUTION I
Circumstantial Evidence

AFTER HIS SCOTTISH CAMPAIGN of 1296 Edward did not return directly to London. In fact, he was not back at Westminster until 17 June of the following year.[1] The stone taken from Scone Abbey had preceded him and was in Westminster Abbey. It was most likely placed near the shrine of St Edward, or Edward the Confessor as he is better known. On the following day the regalia of Scotland – the gold crown and sceptre– were offered up to St Edward at the shrine.[2] It seemed that the king also intended the stone to be an offering to his name saint, but perhaps when it had been suitably embellished. It was around this time that he ordered a bronze chair to display it.[3]

The commission was given to Adam, his goldsmith, and the bill for the work still survives.[4] Here's a summary:

St Edward the Confessor's shrine in Westminster Abbey.

*For a throne of wood made as a model for the other throne which was to be cast in copper.
£5 0s 0d.*

*For 1500 pounds of copper, and also tin for the alloy.
£12 5s 0d.*

*For payment to a worker who made templates and moulds for the chair, and for casting it.
£10 0s 0d.*

For payment to various workers who worked on the chair after casting, through June and July. £9 7s 11d.

*For tools and the repair of tools.
£2 0s 0d*

The figures above add up to a total of £38 12s 11d. It would be difficult to convert this into a contemporary equivalent but some idea can be gained from the fact that at today's prices the metal alone would cost somewhere in the region of £10,000. At this time an English knight was paid two shillings a day (£38 12s 11d would be enough to hire his services for over a year).[5]

The bill dates from 1300. Although the work was obviously well under way, the total should not be

Edward I from a late thirteenth-century woodcut.

seen as a final price for the job because Adam's bill also tells us that at the end of July 1297, '... work ceased completely by order of the king by reason of his passage to Flanders'.

It may be that Edward wanted to oversee each stage of the work in person. Considering what he was prepared to pay, this would not have been surprising, and might indicate some sort of personal interest in the stone. Aside from its political importance as a symbol of his sovereignty over Scotland, there are grounds for believing that Edward saw it as something of a holy relic. He was a man with a great fondness for relics, numbering among his collection two lumps of rock from Calvary, two pieces of the true cross and a thorn from the crown of Christ.[6]

If the legend which tells of the stone being brought to Scotland by Scota, the daughter of an Egyptian pharaoh, and the other one which identifies it with Jacob's pillow were current in Scotland at this time – and this seems to have been the case – then their acceptance by Edward could only have assisted the stone's elevation towards relic status.[7]

A more mundane explanation might be found in the fact that at the same time Edward called a halt to a number of other royal works.[8] Perhaps multitasking wasn't his strongest suit.

The king left Westminster on 30 July and was in Flanders before the end of August. Included in his army were Scottish prisoners who had been captured at Dunbar. For Edward, it was standard practice to use the remnants of defeated armies in succeeding campaigns. He had used Irish troops in Wales and in Scotland, and Welsh troops in Scotland. Now he proposed to use Irish, Welsh and Scottish troops in Flanders.[9] Those prisoners who agreed to serve with him were set free on parole. There had been quite an extensive bag at Dunbar. The top of the list reads as follows:

Earls
Ross, Atholl and Menteith.
Barons or Sons of Barons
John Comyn the younger, aka the Red Comyn
Richard Siward

PROSECUTION I: CIRCUMSTANTIAL EVIDENCE

John Moubray
Andrew Murray
John of Inchmartin
David Graham
Alexander Menzies
Nicholas Randolph.[10]

The earl of Menteith had been released earlier and probably accompanied Edward on his tour round Scotland.[11] The others were sent to the Tower of London. The list continues with the names of over a hundred men who represented negotiable currency. These were sorted into batches of six and sent to castles all over England.

Of the men named above, most took up the king's offer, the most notable being the earl of Atholl and John Comyn. They were freed on the 30 July, the day Edward left Westminster. The earl of Menteith, considering his privileged position, can hardly have had any choice but to volunteer. The earl of Ross remained in the Tower, receiving an allowance of sixpence a day. Andrew Murray and Nicholas Randolph also stayed and got fourpence each.[12] The lesser men seemed to have followed their leaders and most of the Scots who went to France were adherents of Atholl, Menteith or Comyn.[13]

Adam the goldsmith was destined never to finish his chair. At some point in 1298 or 1299 Edward cancelled the bronze project and gave the order for the wooden chair which stands in the abbey today.[14] The new chair was made by Walter of Durham. He is described as the king's painter, but would also have had skills as a furniture maker and the authority to employ other craftsmen. The chair was completed by 27 March 1300.[15]

This sudden change of mind cannot simply be passed off as part of an economy drive. A glance at Adam's bill above shows that the project must have been some considerable way towards completion. All that could be realised by putting a stop to it would have been the scrap value of the metal. It is questionable whether the cost of a new wooden chair, painted and gilded as it was, could have been met within this budget.[16]

The Coronation Chair today. The stone was returned to Scotland in 1996.

It has also been suggested that Edward cancelled the bronze chair because he was concerned about its weight, both in terms of moving it and possible damage to the intricate Cosmati mosaic pavement which goes round the front and sides of St Edward's shrine. To this it could be said that a man brought up in knightly skills might have had some idea of the weight of metal, and if it didn't occur to him as a concern, Adam the goldsmith would have pointed it out. Failing this, some sort of dais could have been constructed to spread the load. As to mobility, we can see from Adam's bill that the bronze chair was to be cast in separate parts, as might be expected. What has been assembled can be taken apart. The chair was intended from the start as being principally for the priest celebrant. Its later use in coronations would be occasional and need not have caused much inconvenience. Finally, there was plain paved space between the pavement and the walls of the chapel to provide a number of alternative locations.[17]

The question which still arises out of all of this is why Edward, having ordered a bronze chair weighing the best part of a ton, and seen it most of the way towards completion, should decide to scrap it in favour of a less triumphalist wooden version.

Perhaps someone told him he had been conned.

We do not have to look very far for suspects. Among the considerable number of Scots who went with him to Flanders were many who would have been familiar with the appearance of the stone at Scone Abbey. The point does not need to be laboured.

Enthronement on the Stone of Scone meant the assumption of kingship and we can take for granted a familiarity with its general appearance, at least among the earls and barons. Some of those in Flanders – Menteith, for instance, who had not been imprisoned – might also have seen the stone which lay in Westminster Abbey. At any rate, it does not require much in the way of descriptive powers to transmit the idea of an oblong sandstone block.

It may just have been that some of the more perceptive of the Scots realised that what they knew of the stone at Scone and of the stone at Westminster didn't tally. Possibly a discreet whisper to this effect reached the royal ear.

That same ear was soon to be troubled by other news: of Stirling Bridge and a sizeable English army cut to pieces, not to mention the flayed skin of Edward's treasurer in Scotland, which was treated in like manner and sent round the country in token of victory. To add insult to injury, as the king turned for home and revenge, the Scots in his army deserted *en masse* and went over to the French. However, the Scots at Stirling Bridge had suffered one significant loss. Andrew Murray, who had raised the north against Edward, died of wounds sustained in the battle. His military training and tactical awareness would be greatly missed.

By July of the following year Edward was in Scotland again. He had come north with serious intent, bringing with him an army of 2,000 horse and 12,000 foot, many of the latter being Welsh and Irish. William Wallace, whose name, to the English, had become a byword for evil since his success at Stirling Bridge and a follow-up raid on Northumberland, chose to meet him 'on hard ground on one side of a hill beside Falkirk'.[18]

To counter the threat of the English heavy cavalry he drew his men up in four vast schiltrons, each a tightly-packed mass of men with their spears pointing out. Round each formation was a further barrier of stakes roped together. The archers filled the spaces in between and the cavalry stood in the rear. There was also some protection offered by the ground itself, with a boggy loch in front, broken ground to each side and Callendar Wood behind.

Wallace, a man remembered as a guerrilla leader, had built

himself a castle. Edward set about tearing it down. The English cavalry moved forward and, discovering the loch, swung out on each side of the Scottish line. This brought them within reach of the Scottish horse, who fled the field without a blow being struck. Deprived of action, the English knights drove through the spaces between the schiltrons, killing the bowmen almost to a man. After this it was just a matter of time.

Before the battle Wallace had said, 'I have brought you to the ring. Dance if you can' – or so the story goes.[19] The picture which comes down is not so much of nimble feet but of hopeless rooted persistence as the Welsh arrows withered the schiltrons and the ranks closed and closed until the heavy English armour moved forward again and trampled them down. Wallace and some others escaped to lick their wounds and Edward went on to Stirling to rest from his exertions. He was slightly injured, not from the battle but due to a horse having trodden on him the previous night.[20]

Edward stayed in Stirling for over two weeks. Around this time, and not later than the 17th, something rather odd happened at Scone. The account which follows is from the abbey records:

> In the name of the Lord, Amen; in the year of His incarnation 1298, in the month of August, the seventeenth day; in the time of Thomas, eleventh abbot of Scone by the mercy of God; concerning the monastery of Scone, which has been destroyed by the efforts of the king of England. The wood carvings in the church, the refectory, the dormitory, the cloister, the treasury, consecrated hosts, the altar, chests, coffins and reliquaries have been battered and broken up, so that wherever in the monastery one looks things are broken, even in its smithy, hall and baptistry.[21]

What happened at Scone has to be seen against the general background, which at this time was rather smoky, for Edward's men were also busy elsewhere: Perth and St Andrews were torched.[22] However, things seem to have been handled rather more gently at

Scone: nothing burnt, nobody killed, just the sort of methodical breaking up and tearing down which might be associated with a rather violent and hasty search. If this was the case, the obvious question to ask is, what were they looking for?

After a progress that took in Carlisle, Durham and Lincoln, Edward returned to Westminster on 13 February 1299. He was there or nearby until April and during this time he may well have ordered the wooden chair which has survived to this day.

Table of Events

8 August 1296	The enthronement stone removed from Scone and sent to Westminster.
17 June 1297	Edward arrives at Westminster.
June 1297	Edward orders a bronze chair to hold the stone.
30 July 1297	Edward leaves for Flanders accompanied by freed Scottish prisoners. Work halted on the bronze chair.
11 September 1297	Battle of Stirling Bridge.
March 1298	Edward returning home. Scots in Flanders go over to the French.
July 22	Battle of Falkirk.
July 26–August 9	Edward at Stirling.
Before August 17	Scone Abbey wrecked.
13 February–23 April 1299	Edward at Westminster.
By 27 March 1300	Wooden chair completed.

Endnotes

1. Edward's arrivals and departures throughout this book conform to those in E W Safford, *Itinerary of Edward I*, 2, 1291–1307 (London: Public Records Office, 1976).
2. Joseph Stevenson (ed), *Documents Illustrative of Sir William Wallace, his Life and Times*, 2:115 (Glasgow: Maitland Club, 1841), pp142, 144.
3. M Dominica Legge, 'La Piere D'Escoce', *Scottish Historical Review*, 38 (1959), p110.
4. National Archives, E101/357/1; Warwick Rodwell, *The Coronation Chair and the Stone of Scone* (Oxford & Oakville: Oxbow Books, 2013), p36.
5. J Nichols (ed), *Liber Quotidianus Contrarotulatoris Garderobae. Anno regni regis Edwardi primi vicesimo octavo*, (1299–1300), (London: Society of Antiquaries, 1787), p60 (see also xli).
6. Joseph Hunter, 'King Edward's spoliations in Scotland in A.D. 1296 – The Coronation Stone – Original and Unpublished Evidence' *Archaeological Journal*, 13, p251; L F Salzman, *Edward I* (London: Constable, 1968), p178; George Watson, 'The Black Rood of Scotland', *Transactions of the Scottish Ecclesiological Society* 2, Part 1 (1906–1907). (Aberdeen: W Jolly, 1907). The Cross of Neith was supposed to contain a fragment of the true cross. Edward took it from Caernarfon in 1283. The Black Rood of Scotland, of similar reputation, had quite recently come into his hands through the campaign of the previous year. The collection was growing.
7. The Scota legend is recounted in an English poem written in or soon after 1307. This is printed and discussed in Legge, 'La Piere D'Escoce'. It seems to be independent of the oldest known Scottish account of the legend, by Baldred Bisset in 1301 (see W F Skene (ed), *Chronicles of the Picts and Scots, and other early memorials of Scottish History* (Edinburgh: H M General Register House, 1867), p280.
8. Richard Welander, David J Breeze, Thomas Owen Clancy (eds), *The Stone of Destiny: Artefact and Icon*, 22 (Edinburgh: Society of Antiquaries Scotland, 2003), p209.
9. Maurice Powicke, *The Thirteenth Century, 1216-1307* (Volume 4 of *The Oxford History of England*) (Oxford: Clarendon Press, 1953), pp384, 565, 678–79; Harry Rothwell (ed), *Chronicle of Walter of Guisborough* (London: Offices of the Royal Historical Society, 1957), p270; Joseph Stevenson (ed), *Documents Illustrative of the History of*

Scotland, 1286–1306 (Edinburgh: H M General Register House, 1870), pp124–26; *Miscellany of the Scottish History Society*, 11 (Edinburgh: Scottish History Society, 1990), pp30–133, *passim*.

10 Joseph Bain (ed), *Calendar of Documents relating to Scotland*, (Edinburgh: HM General Register House, 1881–1888), 2:742.

11 Bain, *Calendar of Documents*, 823, p195, states that the earl of Menteith swore fealty to Edward at Elgin, having previously been released from prison, 'by the king's grace'.

12 Bain, *Calendar of Documents*, 2:888, 939, 940, 1027.

13 G W S Barrow, *Robert Bruce and the Community of the Realm of Scotland*, 4th edition (Edinburgh: Edinburgh University Press, 2005), p128, n41.

14 Rodwell, *Coronation Chair*, p38.

15 J Nichols (ed), *Liber Quotidianus Contrarotulatoris Garderobae. Anno regni regis Edwardi primi vicesimo octavo*, (1299–1300), (London, 1787), 60, (see also xli). This bill, for £1 19s 7d is not for the chair itself but for making a covering and making and decorating a step for it. The bill itself is not dated but occurs between items dated 20 and 23 May. It states that the wooden chair was ordered by the king in March. Adam's bill tells us that the stone was set in the wooden chair by 27 March.

16 Rodwell, *Coronation Chair*, p37.

17 Rodwell, *Coronation Chair*, pp37–41.

18 H Rothwell (ed) *Chronicle of Walter of Guisborough* (London,1957), p327.

19 Henry T Riley (ed), *Chronica Willelmi Rishanger*, (London, Rolls Series, 1865), p187, '*I have browghte ȝowe to the ryng, hoppe ȝef ȝe kunne*'.

20 This account of the Battle of Falkirk is derived from Barrow, *Robert Bruce*, pp132–36.

21 *Liber Ecclesie de Scon*, (Edinburgh: Bannatyne Club, 1843), 89:124. [Translated by Gilbert Markus.]

22 Rothwell, *Walter of Guisborough*, p328.

PROSECUTION II
Eyewitness Evidence

ON 15 FEBRUARY 1951, at the height of the controversy following the removal of the stone from Westminster Abbey by four Glasgow students, an article by James S Richardson, a former HM Inspector of Ancient Monuments for Scotland, appeared in *The Scotsman* newspaper. In the course of a discussion of the stone Richardson turned his attention to the Great Seals of the early Scottish kings. His observations are worth quoting:

> The Great Seal of Alexander I, the founder of the Abbey of Scone, and those of David I (1124–1153) and William the Lion (1165–1214), show the King seated on an altar-like stool, which might well be a stone chair set on the floor, and in the words of Fordun, 'decked with silken cloths interwoven with gold'. On the seat is a well-stuffed cushion covered with fine fabric, and there is a footstool appropriately decked. Certainly, the representation shows a stool more than eleven inches high; and no king could sit with dignity on a stone, firmly set upon the land of his kingdom if it were only eleven inches in height.

Alexander I
r. 1107–1124

David I
r. 1124–1153

William the Lion
r. 1165–1214

Richardson goes on to discuss later seals:

> As regards the representations of Alexander III and John Balliol, however, the Great Seals appear to indicate that, by their time, the stone chair was covered by a wooden one richly decorated in the Gothic manner.

Alexander III, second seal
r. 1249–1286

John Balliol
r. 1292–1296

Certainly any examination of the seals quickly reveals a style of seating which is totally at odds with the stone Edward took from Scone Abbey. Unfortunately, Richardson does not appear to have looked further afield than Scone when considering possible influences on the design of seals.

From the reign of William the Conqueror through to that of Henry III the English seals conform fairly much to a type. There is development and some individual variation but certain elements remain consistent. The king is always depicted sitting on a backless stool with a sword in his right hand and an orb in the left.[1]

William the Conquerer
r. 1066–1087

Henry III, first seal
r. 1216–1272

This pattern was more or less faithfully copied in the northern kingdom, as the first seal of Alexander III shows.

Alexander III, first seal.   Alexander III, second seal.

In the second extract quoted Richardson suggests that by the time of Alexander III the stone chair had acquired a wooden cover. Certainly Alexander's second seal is significantly more elaborate than his first and all the seals of his predecessors. The chair has become wider and for the first time it has a thick back which rises to roughly the level of the king's shoulders. The whole construction is, as Richardson says, 'richly decorated in the Gothic manner'.

However, once again we find that the influence comes from the south rather than from Scone, in this case from the second seal of Henry III.

It is tempting to attribute the major advance in design which this seal represents as being due to Henry's twin love of the arts and of France. It was, after all, this king who was responsible for the rebuilding of Westminster Abbey in the French Gothic style. However, there are no French seals in a style remotely resembling this one.

Second seal of Henry III.

Seal of Richard, King of the Romans.

In fact, Henry's seal is not so much a case of transfusion but rather of transplant. It is based on the seal used by the contemporary King of the Romans – in effect, king of Germany – who just happened to be Henry's younger brother, Richard of Cornwall. How greatly Henry was impressed by his brother's achievement remains obscure. He certainly seems to have been impressed by his seal. In only slightly altered form it begins to appear on English documents within two years of Richard's election in January 1257.[2]

Like all previous designs used by English kings it travelled north, possibly being adopted in Scotland when Alexander reached his majority in 1262. It is thus to the court at Aachen rather than the abbey at Scone that we should look for the origins of this change of design.

Aside from the royal seals, there is one more which is worth looking at. This is the later seal of Scone Abbey, which depicts the coronation of the king of Scots. He is shown sitting on a throne, crowned and holding a sceptre in his right hand. He is attended by seven figures. The two in the foreground, probably the bishop of St Andrews and the abbot of Scone, are adjusting his robe.

The problem with this seal is that it seems to date from the fourteenth century and so comes too late for our purposes. It may, as Richardson suggests in the article quoted, be modelled on an older matrix. It is equally possible that the loss of the stone brought about a change of style, or quite possibly that the depiction was never intended to be realistic in the first place.

Unfortunately, although there are some examples of earlier Scone seals, there is no surviving example of this type which would allow us to make a comparison. Even if we assume that the style is derivative, the seal tells us very little. Most of the seat is hidden by the king's robes and what is revealed could be a stone, or a cushion on a stone, or a cushion on a stool, or a stone inside a stool, or almost any combination of the three.

A final pictorial example mentioned by Richardson is a miniature of David I and his grandson Malcolm IV, both seated, which fills up the space inside the letter M in the charter of Kelso Abbey. Richardson suggests that the seat occupied by David I:

exhibits at the exposed top corner a volute, apparently in stone, a feature which, with Guisborough's description [a description provided by the fourteenth-century chronicler, Walter of Guisborough], suggests a Roman altar, the hollowed-out and round part being the basin; and we should remember that the Abbey of Scone was built within easy reach of a Roman bridge and the three Roman camps of Bertha, Gold Castle and Grassy Walls.

According to art historian, Linda Reynolds, formerly Department of Extra-Mural Studies, University of Edinburgh and currently Associate Professor of Art History at Florida University's Florence Program:

> The miniatures of David I and his grandson Malcolm IV in the Kelso Charter of 1159 are typical of the medieval stylised image of the ruler. The ultimate source of these figures is to be found in Byzantine images of Christ as the emperor.
>
> The artists of the day were monks. Moving from one religious centre to another they took their native styles with them and were themselves influenced by the different styles they encountered. The Kelso miniaturist is working firmly within this tradition. Nothing which he paints has not been painted before; indeed the images are hackneyed, even degenerate. To go back to an ultimate source, the following

watered-down Byzantine influences are to be seen:

The full-frontal position (often used for Byzantine emperors), the elongation of the body between shoulder and hip and the large frontally staring eyes.

Both figures sit on cushioned stools, the ends of the cushion bulging up on either side to show the weight of the bodies. Often, in Byzantine art, Christ or the emperor was shown sitting on a cushioned stool rather than the high-backed throne which tends to be associated in the West with images of kingship. Occasionally in the West the stool would be shown on an arcaded pedestal, and the round-topped vertical markings under the thrones are a crude attempt to show the spaces between the arcades.

What has happened is that the Kelso miniaturist, working from a pattern book or from a miniature, has failed to understand the conventions of perspective and has misread this as a simple pattern.

The perspective of the stools is a crude and diluted version of the deliberate non-perspective of Byzantine art, which was not interested in a three-dimensional representation of reality. From this comes the slithering forward effect of David and Malcolm and the way their feet hover insubstantially over the pedestal of the stools. They are actually meant to be placed on them rather than over them.

...The above analysis does not mean that the Kelso artist looked at Byzantine sources directly but rather that, behind what appears to be a typical medieval image there is in fact a much older tradition. The miniature is certainly of historic interest but from the artistic point of view it has little merit. The execution is hackneyed and clumsy. The artist paints nothing which is new. He is working very firmly within the format of representations of the ruler.[3]

Early sixth century Byzantine mosaic from the church of San Vitale, Ravenna, Italy, showing Christ as the emperor.

There seems to be no reason to go further than Reynolds' analysis in order to explain the content of the Kelso miniature and any ideas we have of relating it to a real object should, however, reluctantly, be abandoned.

It would seem that there is no pictorial evidence whatsoever as to the appearance of the stone which lay in Scone Abbey up till the summer of 1296.

Endnotes

1 On seals, see Walter de Gray Birch, *History of Scottish Seals from the Eleventh to the Seventeenth Century* (Stirling: Mackay; London: Fisher Unwin, 1905–1907), 1–2; Henry Laing, *Descriptive Catalogue of Impressions from Ancient Scottish Seals* (Edinburgh: Constable, 1850) and supplement (1856); Alfred and Alan Wyon, *The Great Seals of England* (London: Chiswick Press, 1887); Walter de Gray Birch, *Catalogue of Seals in the Department of Manuscripts in the British Museum* (London: Longmans, 1887–1900), 5: France, 6: Germany.

See also https://www.mernick.org.uk/seals/index.htm.

2 Richard, earl of Cornwall, obtained the votes of four of the seven electors. The other three went to Alfonso X of Castile. Although Richard was crowned king of the Romans in Charlemagne's chair at Aachen, the divided vote and lack of total support prevented his investiture as Holy Roman Emperor in Rome. It is worth noting that his seal makes no effort to represent the throne at Aachen, which, though an impressive structure of white Carrara marble, is clean-lined and simple in design.

3 Personal Communication with Linda Reynolds.

PROSECUTION III
Eyewitness Testimony

THE DIFFERENCE BETWEEN the appearance of the stone taken from Scone Abbey in 1297 and the descriptions in various 'ancient chronicles' has been noticed by more than one observer. As early as 1781 this caused an interchange of views in the staid pages of *The Gentleman's Magazine*.[1]

Typical of the type of description at issue is that given by the fourteenth-century Scottish chronicler, John of Fordun, who speaks of 'a marble chair, sculptured in very antique workmanship by a careful artist'.[2] We should, however, perhaps treat this with a certain amount of caution. Although Fordun is known to have made use of earlier sources, his chronicle was not compiled until the late 1300s, almost a century after the stone left Scone. His work can fairly be described as an ancient chronicle but it hardly qualifies as a contemporary account.

In fact, although later descriptions abound, there is only one from the period in question which might be seen as credible. It occurs in the pages of Walter of Guisborough's chronicle and reads as follows:

> On St Andrew's Day the same John Balliol was made king of Scotland according to the custom of the Scots, which follows. At the monastery of Scone was placed a very large stone in the church of God, near the great altar, somewhat concave, shaped in the manner of a round chair, in which future kings were placed, according to custom, as the place of their coronation.

The date referred to was 30 November 1292. The report was written either in 1300 or very soon afterwards.[3]

This chronicle, which comes from an Augustinian priory in north Yorkshire, is largely a result of compilation from other sources. In the area of Anglo-Scottish affairs between 1291 and 1300 what Walter of Guisborough writes is quite closely related to another account, which itself may originate from a monastic house in the north of England.[4]

However, when we compare the two we find a rather interesting difference. The description of the stone above appears only in Guisborough. The other account merely refers to John Balliol's enthronement. Guisborough, by contrast, not only describes the appearance of the stone but follows it with a fairly detailed description of the enthronement ceremony. After this the two accounts merge together again with a reference to John Balliol doing homage to Edward I on 26 December of the same year.

Since the material on the stone and the enthronement ceremony is only found in Guisborough, it becomes relevant to ask where it came from.[5] According to Harry Rothwell, the editor of the most recent edition of the chronicle, neither account derives from the other. It is more likely that the two share a common source, since lost, which has been abridged in the other account and expanded from other sources in Guisborough.

With regard to these sources, Rothwell says:

> Much in the interstices between the borrowings...can also be accounted for: either as documents or events of common knowledge or as matters a Guisborough chronicler could have special knowledge of or interest in.[6]

We can ignore 'documents'. These appear from time to time in the chronicle but need not concern us here. This leaves us with 'special knowledge' or 'interest'.

Now it may be that the size and shape of an enthronement stone in an Augustinian abbey in Scotland was well-known to the inhabitants of an Augustinian priory in Yorkshire, and it's worth mentioning here that the original priory at Scone had been founded by monks from Yorkshire – and, as Rothwell says, 'In the case of Scotland, monasteries, as we know, were required to both give and receive information'.[7]

This in itself does not account for the chronicler's obvious interest in what happened there in 1292.[8] There is in fact a closer connection, this being that at some time between 1119 and 1124 Guisborough priory was founded by the local lord of the manor, one Robert de Brus.[9]

At the time he was lord of Cleveland and not long afterwards he was granted the lordship of Annandale by David I of Scotland. Becoming a Scottish lord did not induce any great change in his loyalties. He remained an Englishman, and a Yorkshireman, till his death and his body was buried in the priory which he had founded. His elder son, Adam, fell heir to the Cleveland lordship.

It was the younger son, Robert, who, having taken over the Annandale land during his father's lifetime, became a real lord of Scotland, committed enough to fight against his father at the Battle of the Standard in 1138. From him descended the long line of Annandale Bruces which eventually was to take the throne of Scotland.[10]

Nevertheless, as G W S Barrow says:

> in general, the Scottish Bruces did not sever their connections with England. They held land in County Durham and family loyalty and piety kept their love for Guisborough Priory so strong that they never tried to found a monastery of their own in Annandale.[11]

The connection worked both ways, in that Guisborough Priory held lands in Annandale.[12] The Bruce connection is obvious from the chronicle, which is studded with complimentary references to various members of the family. It can thus be readily seen how Balliol's enthronement would have been of direct interest to the inhabitants of the priory, following as it did on the settlement of the long succession dispute between John Balliol and Robert the Bruce, the grandfather of the future king. Had the decision gone the other way the priory might have seen its benefactor enthroned as king of Scots.

Given this close link with the Bruce family and a consequent direct interest in the succession to the Scottish throne, it is surely not beyond the bounds of possibility that this description of the stone was based on eyewitness accounts. Bruces would have been readily encountered at Guisborough and among them we can surely assume some familiarity with the stone on which the head of the family hoped to be enthroned.

We can go a little further than this. On 25 March 1295, less than three years after his rival's enthronement as king of Scots, old Robert the Bruce the Competitor died at Lochmaben. Like all previous lords of Annandale he was interred at Guisborough Priory, '...beside his father, on the second Sunday after Easter, the 17th of April, with great honour, as was befitting, and great reverence'.[13] One would expect the family to have been in attendance. As mentioned earlier, the description of the stone was written comparatively soon afterward.

In a sense this point does not have to be laboured. Examining the Guisborough account because it is contemporary does not detract from the fact that all later accounts describe the stone which was at Scone in terms of which are totally incompatible with the stone which was taken to Westminster.[14] Whatever the reliability of the sources of these later works, the fact remains that no alternative point of view was ever put forward. There is quite simply no mediaeval description which can be taken to refer, however, obliquely, to an oblong block of sandstone.

Traditionally these later works have been allowed more credence than has been granted here, and various theories have been advanced to overcome the disparity between the descriptions and the object in question. Let's examine a couple of these theories:

> *The stone was originally shaped like a chair but Edward's workmen knocked the sides and back off it in order to make it fit the recess in the bronze chair which had been designed to hold it.*[15]

In order to accept this we have to believe that a chair-shaped stone was reduced to an oblong in order to fit it into a chair, which seems rather illogical to say the least.

There is also the question of whether the king would have turned the heavy squad loose on an object which he seems – at least originally – to have venerated enough to offer to a saint.

We might consider the fact that Adam's bill specifically states that the bronze chair was constructed 'for putting on the stone on which the kings of Scotland were crowned'. Considering the cost of the project, and the type of man he was working for, it seems unlikely that Adam would have gone ahead and produced a chair of completely the wrong design.

Also, the top surface of the stone is unfinished, having the surface of the original sandstone layer. Knocking the sides and back off it would have left traces.

> *The stone was always oblong but whilst at Scone it was contained in a chair which was left behind by the removal team.*[16]

This one was put forward by John Stuart over a century ago. As authority for it he cites Fordun; the reference is to the investiture of Robert the Bruce in 1306. This was the first such occasion at Scone since the stone had been removed and some sort of substitute would have been required. According to Fordun, Bruce was, '…set on the royal throne … in the manner in which the kings of Scots were wont to be invested'.[17]

Stuart takes this 'royal throne' to refer to a chair which had contained the stone up till its removal ten years before. The article in which Stuart advanced this theory appeared as a sort of supplement to a longer piece by William F Skene. Stuart admits to not having seen Skene's work before publication. This is unfortunate because Stuart's premise is unwittingly but utterly squashed in Skene's article.

Skene refers initially to a line from the Acts of Parliament of Scotland which reads, 'the king sitting, as is usual, in the royal seat on the Mount of Scone'.[18] He goes on to say, 'This *'Sedes Regia'* must not be confounded with the stone seat, which was used at the coronation only, and was kept in the Abbey Church, to which the name of *'Cathedra'* is always applied. The royal seat here referred to was placed on the Moot Hill, and was used when the king presided at a parliament or court of justice. It was on this seat on the Moot Hill that Robert the Bruce was crowned in 1306, *'in sede positus regalia'* (placed in the royal seat) after the seat called the *'Cathedra'*, or stone, had been removed to England'.[19]

It is also worth noting that Fordun himself uses the word *cathedra* (chair) when referring to all previous enthronements. Only when he comes to Robert the Bruce does this change to *sedes regalis* (royal seat). Whatever authority Fordun has cannot be used to back an argument for a conveniently discarded chair.

Aside from this, we are still faced with Walter of Guisborough, who does not talk of a chair containing a stone but of 'a very large stone...hollowed out like a round chair'.

It may also be significant that in the original Latin he uses the words *lapis pergrandis*, a very large stone. However, when the stone is recorded in the English royal inventories it has shrunk somewhat, being now merely a *petra magna*, a large stone.[20]

At some point in its history, and possibly in Westminster, the stone was reduced in size, but this can only have amounted to centimetres – hardly enough to justify a change from *pergandis* to *magna*.[21]

Maybe we should take a closer look at the stone today and what this can tell us.

At some point before 1819 the stone was identified as being Scottish Lower Old Red Sandstone of Devonian Age by John

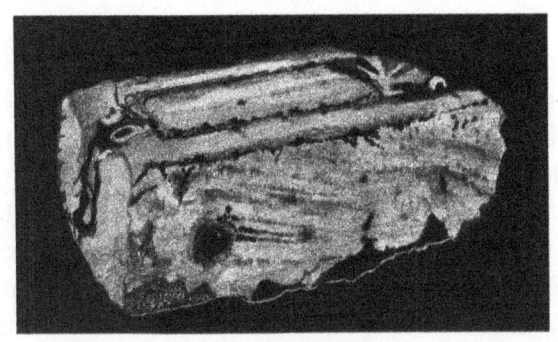

The Westminster Stone.

MacCullock, one of Scotland's early geologists. This excluded its origin in Ireland, Egypt or anywhere else. MacCullock, furthermore, stated that it resembled stone used in Dunstaffnage Castle, suggesting that it came from western Scotland.[22]

In 1865 Sir Andrew Ramsay, director of the Geological Survey of England, examined the stone and came to the conclusion that it consists of:

> ...a dull reddish or purple sandstone, with a few embedded pebbles. One of these is of quartz, and two others of a dark material, the nature of which I was unable to ascertain. They may be Lydian stone. The rock is calcareous, and is of the kind that masons would call 'freestone'.[23]

Not long after this the stone was examined in more detail by Archibald Geikie, director of the newly-formed Geological Survey of Scotland. He concluded that it came from 'one of the sandstone districts between the coasts of Argyll and the mouths of the Tay and Forth'. Though this would still allow for it coming from Dunstaffnage he also wrote:

> I do not see any evidence in the stone itself why it may not have been taken from the neighbourhood of Scone; indeed it perfectly resembles some of the sandstones of that district.[24]

This was confirmed in 1937 when Professor CF Davidson examined the microscopic structure of the stone and pointed out that it differed significantly from the stones of Dunstaffnage, and narrowed its origin down to Perthshire, not far from Scone.[25]

In the wake of the Westminster Stone's removal in 1950, Davidson, then Senior Principal Geologist, HM Geological Survey, remarked in the *Illustrated London News* that the most microscopic tests had failed to find any difference between it and the rocks in the Scone area.[26]

In 1996 the stone was returned to Scotland. In 1998, after a detailed re-examination by the British Geological Survey, it was concluded that Lower Old Red Sandstone of this type was most similar to that of the Scone Formation, which surrounds the site of the abbey.[27] There are two outcrops of similar stone near the abbey, one by the River Tay, and one beside the Annaty Burn, which runs into it. The lower part of the burn is called Quarrymill and the name derives from this having been the site of quarries and mills dating back to the Middle Ages. It is most likely that the stone, and the other stones of Scone Abbey, came from here.

The stone measures 430 mm from front to back. It is 710 mm wide and 265 mm high. It weighs 152 kg.[28] The upper and lower surfaces haven't been dressed and show the original forms of the sandstone bed from which it was taken. The upper surface has seen some wear, particularly towards the back. The tops of the vertical sides have been dressed and the front edge is still quite clean. The stone tapers slightly from top to bottom. Large flakes have been detached around the bottom edge. Most of these seem to have been made with hammer blows. On the right-hand side at the back there is a fracture caused when the stone was removed from Westminster Abbey in 1950. This follows the lines of an existing crack in the stone. The back left corner has been chipped, possibly during the same operation.

A rectangular outline has been roughly cut into the upper surface. This is presumably the beginnings of a recess to house a commemorative plaque. The work may have been abandoned when a wooden seat board was later placed above the stone in Westminster Abbey. Also on the front, towards the back, two crosses have been cut into the surface. There is no explanation for these beyond perhaps medieval graffiti. Also on the lower front face are two obvious and one faint indentations. These correspond with gaps in the framework of the coronation chair and seem to have been caused by visitors scraping off sand from the stone, simply as a souvenir or for its religious associations.

On each side an iron ring is attached to a staple with a figure-of-eight link. Above these, rough housings have been cut into the stone so that they can lie flush with the surface when in the upper position. As to their purpose, we might immediately dismiss the idea that they were fitted by Edward's workmen at Scone so that the stone could be slung from a pole and moved by two men, or possibly horses. There would have been no need for this. The standard way to move a stone of this size is on a mason's barrow, then presumably onto a cart for the 440 miles to London. When the stone was found at Arbroath Abbey in 1951 after being hidden in Scotland, it was on a mason's barrow.

There is also the fact that the staples for the rings are placed below the centre of gravity. If slung onto a pole the stone would have been unstable and a nightmare to carry. Cutting recesses above the rings would counter this tendency to topple over, but why go to all this trouble rather than just put the stone on a barrow? Thousands of other stones of roughly this size would have been moved in the construction of Scone Abbey, and all without rings.

This leaves us with two main possibilities, both based on the rings having another purpose, both expressed in published works.

Warwick Rodwell, writing in *The Coronation Chair and the Stone of Scone,* takes the view that the rings were installed in Westminster Abbey and placed below the mid-line in order to help chain the stone to the floor. The chronicle of Geoffrey le Baker, which is contemporary, mentions that the stone was secured in this way, though not when the rings were fitted. This might have been done in 1328 when Edward III issued a writ ordering the stone to be sent back to Scotland. This was resisted by the abbot and the people of London.[29]

However, it could be said that to dig holes into the sides of the stone then secure fixings with molten lead is perhaps not the most respectful or cost-effective way of protecting what was regarded as a war trophy and at least locally as a sacred relic.

And to what effect? A couple of crowbars or files could liberate the stone in a fairly short time. Would it not be simpler and involve less damage to said sacred object to keep it in a place of safety within the abbey? If the rings were already in place, however, chaining it down might have been seen as a viable option.

Rodwell also suggests that in the years, possibly hundreds of years, before the seat board was placed above the stone, the wear could have been caused by the stone being sat upon by the priest celebrant, as it regularly was when not used for coronations. This doesn't account for the fact that the wear on the top surface extends from side to side and is greater towards the back. In *Scotland's Stone of Destiny* Nick Aitchison argues that the stone was shaped to fit a recess in Scone Abbey floor, possibly housing religious relics.[30] This would explain the dressing around the top edge. It would seem that if the stone was intended for building, the mason would have dressed its edges rather further in. Additionally, if the stone was simply set into the floor of Scone Abbey, we would expect fairly even wear across the surface before it went south, then further wear towards the front caused by the sitting of successive abbots of Westminster.

The greater wear towards the back is still puzzling.

A possible explanation could be that the recess was before a wide step in the floor, as might be expected before the altar, or it was close to the altar itself. There would be footfall towards the back as people mounted the step or approached the altar and they might also have walked across the stone, from one side of the church to the other.

Moreover, placing the staples lower down would allow for larger rings and thus more purchase for the hands of those lifting the stone out of its recess. Tapering would also be helpful when moving it out of and back into the recess.

During examination of the stone by Historic Environment Scotland in April 2023, prior to the coronation of King Charles III, X-ray fluorescence analysis discovered traces of copper alloy on the stone's top surface, coinciding with a dark stain near the centre. This suggested contact with a bronze or brass object.[31]

Reliquaries were often made of these alloys and one such might well have been placed on top of the stone after they were lifted out of the recess. Furthermore, during religious festivals these might have stayed together for some time. It can be assumed that this staining occurred while the stone was at Scone as there is no explanation for it afterwards.

All in all, if protecting a relic was the original purpose of the stone which went south in 1297, the abbot of Scone would have had a possible substitute with saintly associations, well-worn by the passage of many feet and perhaps conveniently close to the altar.

Endnotes

1. *The Gentleman's Magazine*, October 1781, 51, pp452–3; 52, pp22–3.
2. William F Skene (ed), Johannis de Fordun, *Chronica Gentis Scotorum*, (Edinburgh: Edmonston & Douglas, 1871–1872), 1: Latin, 2: English translation, 2:23, '*marmorea cathedra, arte vetustissima diligenti sculptum opifice*', 1:23.
3. Rothwell, *Walter of Guisborough*, pp238–39. '*Die vero sancti Andree apostoli idem Johannes Balliolus effectus est rex Scocie more Scottorum qui sequitur. Apud monasterium de Scone positus erat lapis pergrandis in ecclesia dei iuxta maius altare concauus quidem et ad modum rotunde cathedra confectus, in quo futuri reges loco quasi coronacionis ponebantur ex more, ...*'. On the date of writing see introduction, ppxxx–xxxi. David H Caldwell, author of *The Stone of Destiny: updating the scholarship*, (Historic Environment Scotland, 2018), p16, has this to say: 'Guisborough deserves to be taken very seriously. He is considered a reliable source for late-13th-century events in the north of Britain, particularly those concerning Anglo-Scottish relations'.
4. Rothwell, *Walter of Guisborough*, pxxvii. The other account appears in British Library Harley manuscript 3860. The relevant portion is in J Stevenson (ed), *Documents Illustrative of Sir William Wallace, his Life and Times* (Glasgow, 1841). 'Extracts from the Harleian Manuscript 3860', f18, b1, pp29–30.
5. An almost identical passage appears in the Riley, *Willelmi Rishanger*, pp162-3. William Rishanger, however, was a monk in St Albans and this part of his chronicle dates from around 1327. It seems likely that he sourced it from Guisborough.
6. Rothwell, *Walter of Guisborough*, pxxvii. The phrase deleted is, 'from these two sources'. The other source has no bearing on this part of the chronicle.
7. Rothwell, *Walter of Guisborough*, pxxvii.
8. A A M Duncan, *Scotland: The Making of the Kingdom* (Edinburgh, Mercat Press, 1975), p131.
9. Rothwell, *Walter of Guisborough*, pxi.
10. Barrow, *Robert Bruce*, pp27–29.
11. Barrow, *Robert Bruce*, p28.
12. Rothwell, *Walter of Guisborough*, pxi.
13. Rothwell, *Walter of Guisborough*, p259.

14 These are discussed in William F Skene, *The Coronation Stone* (Edinburgh: Edmonston & Douglas, 1869). This is more accessible in its original periodical form in *Proceedings of the Society of Antiquaries of Scotland*, 8, to which succeeding page references relate. See also W Douglas Simpson, *Dunstaffnage Castle and the Stone of Destiny* (Edinburgh, Oliver & Boyd, 1958), pp101–36.

15 George Watson, 'The Coronation Stone of Scotland', *Transactions of the Scottish Ecclesiological Society*, 1, pp26–27. A W Clapham puts forward a largely similar theory in *The Antiquaries Journal*, 22, p161. John Stuart, 'Note on the Coronation Stone', *Proceedings of the Society of Antiquaries of Scotland*, 8, pp101–2.

16 Hunter, 'King Edward's Spoliations', p250. See also Stuart, 'Note on the Coronation Stone', pp101–2; Watson, 'The Black Rood of Scotland'.

17 Skene, *Chronica Gentis Scotorum*, 2:333: '*in sede positus regali, modo quo reges Scociae solebant insignari*', 1:340.

18 '*Rege sedente in Sede Regia super montem de Scone ut est moris.*' T Thomson and C Innes (eds), *The Acts of the Parliament of Scotland*, (Edinburgh, Record Commission, 1814–1875), 1:181.

19 Skene, *Coronation Stone*, p28, n1.

20 Stuart, 'Note on the Coronation Stone', pp101–2.

21 Welander, *The Stone of Destiny*, pp18–19.

22 Rodwell, *Coronation Chair*, p26.

23 A P Stanley, *Historical Memorials of Westminster Abbey* (London, John Murray, 3rd edition, 1869) pp594–95.

24 Skene, *Coronation Stone*, p50.

25 Rodwell, *Coronation Chair*, p26.

26 C F Davidson, 'The Stone of Destiny', *The Illustrated London News*, 13 January 1951.

27 Welander, *The Stone of Destiny*, pp33–40.

28 For details of the stone in its current form see Rodwell, *Coronation Chair* and Welander, *The Stone of Destiny*, pp11–32.

29 Rodwell, *Coronation Chair*, pp109–16.

30 Nick Aitchison, *Scotland's Stone of Destiny* (Stroud: The History Press, 2nd edition, 2009), pp53–55. Peter Hill also put forward the idea of the stone having been used as a step in Welander, *The Stone of Destiny*, p20. See also the views of Andy Hopkins and other stonemasons.

31 *The Scotsman*, 5 April 2023.

BACKGROUND II

July 1298 to June 1314

WILLIAM WALLACE escaped from the slaughter of Falkirk but his days as a leader were over. In his place, two Guardians were appointed – Robert the Bruce, grandson of the claimant to the throne of 1291-2, and John Comyn the younger of Badenoch. It was an uneasy partnership which soon burst into open hostility. To reduce the tension, Bishop Lamberton of St Andrews was appointed chief Guardian. Some time later Bruce either resigned or was squeezed out and his place was given to a Comyn associate.

In the summer of 1300 Edward invaded Galloway and defeated a Scottish force at the River Cree. Early in 1305 the king invaded Scotland again. He bypassed Stirling Castle, crossing the Forth on prefabricated pontoon bridges. Wallace was captured in August. He was tried at Westminster and sent to a traitor's death at Smithfield. Unlike many of those who fought against Edward and were forgiven, Wallace had never sworn fealty. By September Edward was at the Moray Firth and in February 1306 the Scots' leaders surrendered.

Robert the Bruce, who had been in the English king's peace for four years, met with John Comyn the younger of Buchan in the Greyfriars' kirk of Dumfries. We do not know the details of their conversation but the result was Bruce stabbing Comyn. Some of his supporters finished off the job. This led to an uprising and Bruce was crowned at Scone on 25 March 1306.

Before the year was out Bruce had been defeated at Methven, near Perth. Fleeing to the west with the remnants of his supporters, he was defeated again by John MacDougall of Argyll at Dail Righ, near Tyndrum. The new king was chased out of his kingdom while his family and many of his supporters met with imprisonment or death. In 1307 Bruce began to fight back. He had two early successes, at Glen Trool and Loudon Hill. That same year Edward died.

Dragging his ailing body north at the head of an expedition designed to subdue the Scots yet again, he breathed his last at Burgh by Sands on the south shore of the Solway, within sight of Scotland.

His son and heir, Edward II, who was urged to continue the project, ran out of resolution at Cumnock and retired to England. He was crowned at Westminster early in 1308. Meanwhile Bruce went about subduing his own enemies in Scotland. He defeated the earl of Buchan at Inverurie and afterwards turned the north-east into a smoking desert. Comyn power was destroyed forever. His next victory, at the Pass of Brander, put paid to the MacDougalls. He then began recapturing the English-held castles.

In 1314 Edward II arrived in Scotland at the head of an imposing army, hoping to draw the Scots into a pitched battle. This happened, at Bannockburn, near Stirling, and he lost. Nonetheless, Edward refused to concede sovereignty over Scotland. The remainder of Bruce's career was to be dominated by the objective of bringing him to the negotiating table in some sort of realistic frame of mind. The devastation of the north of England was the most effective means available.

DEFENCE I

John Walwayn's Testimony

*That at a meeting at York towards the end
of 1324, the Scots asked for the Westminster Stone
to be returned to them.*

THE SOURCE FOR THIS is a contemporary work entitled *The Life of Edward the Second*. The relevant passage reads as follows:

> When they had come there, that is the King of England on the one hand and certain Scottish magnates on the other, the Scots demanded that Scotland should be for ever exempt and free from every exaction of the English kingdom, and they demanded by right of conquest and lordship the whole land they had traversed as far as the gates of York.
> There was also a certain barony in Essex which Robert Bruce had long ago forfeited on account of his rebellion; Robert demanded that this should be restored to him, with the profits, moreover, that the king had received from it in the meantime.
> The Scots also demanded that the royal stone should be restored to them, which the elder King Edward had long ago taken from Scotland and placed at Westminster by the tomb of St Edward. This stone was of famous memory amongst the Scots because on it the kings of Scotland used to receive the government of the kingdom with the sceptre. Scota, daughter of pharaoh brought this stone with her from the country of Egypt ... etc.
> To improve the treaty and strengthen the peace, Robert Bruce proposed that his daughter should be joined in marriage with the king's son.[1]

Obviously, if this were a true account of the proceedings it would count strongly against the substitution theory. After all, nobody would make any effort to repossess a fake.

Unfortunately, since no other report of this meeting has survived, there can be no direct way of establishing whether the statement about the stone is true or false. What we can do, however, is examine the rest of the account to see if it makes sense in terms of the contemporary situation. We can also try to establish who the writer was and whether or not he was present at York, or likely to have had access to a reliable report of the proceedings.

In order to do this we first need to place the meeting in some sort of context.

Rumours of Peace

Bruce's foreign policy could best be summed up in terms of his earlier promise to Edward's father to defend himself with the longest stick he had.[2] Aided by a competent staff which included such talents as James Douglas – known variously as 'the Good' or 'the Black' – and Thomas Randolph, he systematically devastated the north of England from the border to the Humber.

It will become apparent later that there was in fact more system than devastation, and it might be pointed out that parts of south-eastern Scotland were included in the target area, but the above definition will serve for the moment. It would probably have seemed accurate enough to those on the receiving end. The following excerpt from what maybe an eye-witness account describes a raid in 1318:

> In the month of May the Scottish army invaded England further than usual, burning the towns of Northallerton and Boroughbridge and sundry other towns on their march, pressing forward as far as the town of Ripon, which town they despoiled of all the goods they could find; and from those who entered the mother church and defended it against the Scottish army they exacted one thousand marks instead of burning the town itself.

After they had lain there three days, they went off to Knaresborough, destroying that town with fire, and, searching in the woods whither the people had fled for refuge with their cattle, they took away the cattle. And so forth to the town of Skipton in Craven, which they plundered first and then burnt, returning through the middle of that district to Scotland, burning in all directions and driving off countless quantity of cattle.[3]

Faced with this sort of behaviour, coupled with indifference in the south, the northern English magnates were forced into conducting their own negotiations with the Scots. In January 1323 Bruce sat down in Lochmaben Castle with Sir Andrew Harclay, earl of Carlisle, and worked out a peace treaty. An interesting feature of the treaty is that Bruce committed himself to paying nearly £27,000 in ten instalments in return for the English Crown renouncing all claim to sovereignty over Scotland.[4] It is difficult to calculate a modern equivalent for this sum but we are probably talking in terms of another three zeroes.

This impressive piece of private enterprise did Harclay no good at all. Edward interpreted it as treason and the earl suffered the penalty; he was hanged, beheaded, disembowelled, and had his entrails burnt and his body chopped up and sent to various parts of the kingdom.[5]

Ironically, Harclay's death helped to bring about what he had tried to achieve because with his death Edward lost the only effective military force in the north.[6] In May of the same year, within three months of the earl's execution, a thirteen-year truce was concluded between the two countries at Bishopthorpe, near York.

It was agreed that no new fortifications would be built on either side of the border, that wardens would be appointed to control crossings and settle disputes and that there would be protection for shipping running up the English coast to trade with Scotland.[7]

It was in an effort to move forward from this truce towards a permanent peace that representatives of the two countries met again at York towards the end of the following year. Unfortunately, these negotiations ran into the brick wall of Edward's refusal to concede sovereignty over Scotland.

Examination

Since the York talks came to nothing, no treaty was drawn up and we can only speculate about the precise agenda. The documentary evidence we have consists of a few 'business' items. There are safe conducts for the Scottish envoys, led by Bishop Lamberton of St Andrews and Thomas Randolph, and there is a list of the English commissioners which is followed by a brief and very limited statement of objectives.[8] There is also a passing reference to the talks in a letter of the following year in which Edward, writing to the Pope, rather petulantly explains his refusal to concede on the sovereignty issue.[9] All we have relating to what was actually discussed at York is contained in the biography of Edward II quoted previously.

If we condense the quotation above we find that the writer says the Scots put five proposals (or demands) on the table. These were that:

    i. The king of England should recognise Scottish sovereignty.
   ii. The Scots should have the freedom of the north of England.
  iii. Bruce's Essex barony should be restored to him.
  iv. The stone should be returned.
   v. Bruce's daughter should be married to Edward's son.

These will be examined in the order of probability, starting with the one least likely to be true.

Item iii: Bruce's Essex barony should be restored to him

It is true that Bruce had owned land in Essex: the estates of Writtle and Hatfield Broad Oak. He had also held far more extensive tracts of land in other counties, in Huntingdonshire in particular, together with a house in London and the manor of Tottenham.[10] That he should have been concerned only about the Essex estates seems rather odd.

The request is also out of tune with Bruce's general policy towards disinherited landowners, which was in essence that no man should hold land on both sides of the border. For Bruce, who was trying to establish recognition of his sovereignty over an independent state, this would have been a logical position. Incidentally, there is no nationality qualification implied here. Among those granted land in Scotland were Pierre Libaud, a Gascon, and Peter of Spalding, an Englishman.[11] The only proviso Bruce held to was that neither king should be forced to restore the lands of one who had fought against him.

This appears in the abortive Bruce-Harclay treaty of 1323 and again as one of Bruce's proposals for what became the Treaty of Edinburgh-Northampton of 1328.[12] Yet in the York report we find Bruce being portrayed as demanding that Edward should do precisely this – restore the lands of one, namely Bruce, who had fought against him.

Another point is that the restoration of the Essex barony could well have involved Bruce in the business of paying feudal homage for it to the king of England, of declaring himself Edward's vassal. This practice had already proved a dangerous embarrassment to former Scottish kings. There is a record of Alexander II doing homage to Edward I for his English lands and maintaining, under considerable pressure, that for Scotland he did homage only to God.[13]

After the untimely death of Margaret of Norway, when Edward was called in to help settle the succession issue, he managed to obtain homage on more than one occasion from the leading magnates of Scotland.[14] And John Balliol's habit of doing homage almost on demand must have been one of the factors which lent particular aptness to his later nickname of Toom Tabard, the empty jacket.[15] It seems unlikely that Bruce, having come through eighteen years of war to shake his country free of English domination, would have been anxious to revive this particular custom.

Finally, and perhaps more fundamental, there is the question of why the king of Scots should be worried about a couple of pieces of land in Essex.

Item v: Bruce's daughter should be married to Edward's son

Bruce had at least one unmarried daughter at this time. However, such a match of a Scottish princess with an English prince goes against what we know of Bruce's intentions. In the treaty he made with Andrew Harclay the previous year he proposed more or less the opposite – his male heir with a girl from Edward's family. This is especially striking since he had no male heir available at the time. His son, David, arrived in March 1324 and was matched up with Edward's younger daughter, Joan of the Tower, by the Treaty of Edinburgh-Northampton of 1328.

Thus we have two treaties running contrary to and bracketing this report of the York meeting.[16] Unless we accept that Bruce was prone to sudden and total reversals of policy, we have to conclude that this report of the York meeting has got its genders crossed.

Item ii: The Scots should have the freedom of the north of England

This is certainly in tune with the state of affairs on the border at the time. This period saw the real start of the border raids, the long fire that was to flicker and flame even into the days when a Scottish king sat in Walter's wooden chair. The legend comes down the centuries – grim warriors, spurs on the table for dinner, blood and death and balefire, and so on.

In actual fact, the Scots went about the terrorisation of the north of England in a manner more reminiscent of the balance sheet than the ballad. In contrast to the spontaneous and rather inefficient practice of riding south and setting fire to everything in sight, Robert the Bruce developed what amounted to an extremely lucrative system of institutionalised blackmail.

County Durham became the principal target. This was partly due to its occupying, from the Scottish point of view, the optimum geographical position. Northumberland, because of its proximity to the border, was almost totally deserted. In 1316 in Hexham, there were only six people living within six manors: in one village a man and his wife, in another a miller and his son. The rest of the population had evacuated themselves to the designated reception areas of Richmond and Cleveland, which were soon overrun with destitute refugees. Yorkshire, by contrast, was too far away to be seriously threatened.

There was another reason for Durham being viewed as the most lucrative prospect, this being its status as a palatinate, which gave it the unity and bureaucratic machinery to collect money and negotiate its own truces with the Scots. Between 1311 and 1327 it arranged at least eight of these, the total extorted over the period being in the region of £5,000.[17] This was at a time when a carpenter might earn fourpence a day.

Over the years a system developed and that proportion of the money which did not come from the church, or was simply seized, was collected on the basis of a village-by-village assessment. This sort of attention to detail can be seen in Bruce's 1314 demand of £2,202 11s 5½d from Cumberland.[18]

Not surprisingly, the north provided very little revenue for the English Crown at this time. In the North Riding of Yorkshire there were 128 villages too ravaged to pay taxes in 1322.[19] Edward actually gave up sending tax assessors into Northumberland, Cumberland and Westmoreland.[20] The revenue from a fifth of his kingdom was going straight into the Scottish treasury.

Nevertheless, there is a great leap from even as dire a situation as this on the ground to its being given the stamp of royal approval as part of a treaty. The final 1328 settlement, though equitable enough, became known throughout England as 'the Shameful Peace'. It can only be imagined how the English people, with the memory of the Hammer of the Scots still fresh in their minds, would have reacted to his son conceding most of the north.

Edward, who had just put down a major revolt at this time, could hardly have been in the mood to touch off another. Neither is it easy to conceive that Bruce, meeting stiff opposition to the concept of his sovereignty over Scotland, would have extended his claim to take in a largish slice of England as well. Some indication of Bruce's attitude to the finer points of territorial demarcation can be gained from the fact that in 1328 he allowed that ownership of the Isle of Man was at least debatable.[21] For him to have put forward the demand reported above would have been uncharacteristic at the very least, in other terms hopelessly unrealistic.

Item i: England should recognise Scottish sovereignty

This should stand. We have the reference to it in Edward's letter to Rome of the following year. It was what Bruce was prepared to pay nearly £27,000 for when he spoke with Andrew Harclay. It formed the basis of the Scottish negotiating position at every peace conference. It would have been, one might say, common knowledge. If we consider that, out of the four items we have considered, this is the only one which seems to fall within the bounds of probability, we might well ask if the writer of this report had any accurate knowledge of what happened in York in 1324. We will go a long way towards answering this question if we manage to identify the person responsible.

The Witness

'The Life of Edward the Second' comes to us only in the form of a transcript made in 1729 by the Oxford antiquary Thomas Hearne from an original manuscript, since lost. Hearne attributed the work to a monk of the Benedictine abbey of Malmesbury. The translator and editor of the 1957 edition, N Denholm-Young, made a case for an alternative author. From the internal evidence of the text he builds up a picture of the man we should be looking for. The description reads as follows:

> ...a West Country lawyer, an authority on Scotland, one familiar with the court, though hating it, one who likes a good bishop, though not a young one, and who hates the papal Curia; hence one who is almost certainly not himself a bishop, though possibly a failed one. The peak of his career should lie between 1315 and 1323, for this is the best part of the work before us, and he should have reason to break off, without revision, at 1326.

DEFENCE I: JOHN WALWAYN'S TESTIMONY

Answering to this description, Denholm-Young produces:

> A Herefordshire lawyer, clerk to the earl of Hereford, whose career was at its peak as a high government official 1315-23, an expert on Scotland, who had been demoted and failed to obtain a bishopric, who retired in January 1324 and was dead in July 1326.

His name was John Walwayn.[22]

If we accept him as the author in question – and the case made is convincing – then we must also accept that he was not present at the York meeting of 1324. The latter part of Walwayn's career was disappointing. His lord, Humphrey de Bohun, earl of Hereford, was one of the most notable of the barons who rose up against Edward II and the Despensers in 1321. He was also, incidentally, the uncle of that Henry de Bohun over whose head Bruce broke his battle-axe at Bannockburn.

By 1322 Edward had gained the upper hand and the earls of Hereford and Lancaster found themselves retreating north, possibly intending to join forces with the Scots. They were met at Boroughbridge by the men of Cumberland under Andrew Harclay. Hereford died in the battle. Lancaster survived to be executed.[23]

Three days before, John Walwayn, as the king's recently appointed keeper of castles, manors and lands in Wales, had been ordered to pull down Hereford's castle of Brecknock. It is not known how he responded but obvious that he must have been in a position of divided loyalty.

Later in 1323 his personal situation worsened, though not out of any suspected disloyalty to the king. Walwayn had held the office of escheator – a sort of Crown representative – south of the Trent from November 1321. From at least 1285 it had been customary to appoint two escheators with the Trent forming the boundary of their jurisdictions. The Despensers, perhaps as part of their general assault on baronial privilege and tradition, had the number increased to eight in 1323.

In consequence, Walwayn had to surrender all except four of his counties. He managed to hold on to Surrey, Sussex, Middlesex and London until 10 January 1324, when he retired. He was still lord of Stoke Edith, near Hereford, and it seems likely that he spent the remainder of his life – less than three years – there working on his memoir. Certainly it appears that what he had left at his death was not a final version.

Wherever he actually was, we can be fairly certain that he was not at the York meeting of late 1324. Being retired, he would have had no reason for attending. To this we might add a strong reason for *not* attending in that prominent on the list of English commissioners are the names of the two Despensers. This pair had been more or less directly responsible for the open rebellion and death of his lord, together with numerous other Herefordshire men, and for Walwayn's own loss of position.[24]

Given that he stayed in Hereford, we find him facing the problem of trying to cover the meeting with no first-hand knowledge, and quite possibly no first-hand reports either, because it was his neighbours and associates, men of the Welsh marches, who had been most active in the revolt of 1321–2. It was the opposition, the victorious king's party, who were running the show at York.

At this point we might refer back rather briefly to the business of the marriage between Bruce's daughter and Edward's son. Walwayn retired in January 1324. Prince David of Scotland was born in March and a proposal for his marriage to Edward's daughter could have been submitted at the meeting later that same year.

It is just possible that Walwayn, in his study in Herefordshire, had not heard of this latest addition to the Bruce family and simply based his account on the children alive at the time of his departure from public affairs. Whatever his reasons, he seems to have come up with a curiously original arrangement.

Conclusion

Out of the four items we have examined, three have been revealed as less than totally credible and the fourth as public knowledge.

The status of the remaining item, Item iv: The Scots asked for the Westminster Stone to be returned, must be judged in relation to this. In general terms, perhaps we should fall in with Denholm-Young's own assessment, that in this part of the memoir the author's zeal seems to have outrun his capacity.[25] At best this is the unsupported testimony of an unreliable source.

Endnotes

1 Wendy R Childs (ed), *Vita Edwardi Secundi: the Life of Edward the Second* (Oxford: Clarendon Press, 2005), pp222–25.

2 E L G Stones, *Anglo-Scottish Relations, 1174–1328: Some selected documents* (Oxford: OUP 1970), 34, p133, *'il se defendroit de plus long bastoun qui'il eust'*.

3 Herbert Maxwell (ed), *The Chronicle of Lanercost 1272–1346* (Glasgow: James MacLehose, 1913), p221.

4 Barrow, *Robert Bruce*, pp323–35.

5 Maxwell, *Chronicle of Lanercost*, p245.

6 Natalie Fryde, *The Tyranny and Fall of Edward II* (Cambridge: CUP, 1979), p158.

7 Thomas Rhymer (ed), *Foedera, Conventiones, Litterae et Cuiuscunque Generis Acta Publica*, 20 volumes (London, 1704–1735), 2:1, pp521, 524.

8 Rhymer, *Foedera, Conventiones, Litterae*, pp577–78.

9 Rhymer, *Foedera, Conventiones, Litterae*, p595.

10 Barrow, *Robert Bruce*, p186.

11 Barrow, *Robert Bruce*, p365.

12 Barrow, *Robert Bruce*, pp324, 331, 352. See also E L G Stones, 'The Anglo-Scottish negotiations of 1327', *Scottish Historical Review*, 30 (1951), pp52–53.

13 Barrow, *Robert Bruce*, p17.

14 Barrow, *Robert Bruce*, pp49–50, pp100–1.

15 On the origin of Balliol's nickname see Grant Simpson, 'Why was Balliol called *Toom Tabard*?' *Scottish Historical Review*, 47 (1968), pp52–53.

16 Barrow, *Robert Bruce*, pp324, 336–37.

17 Jean Scammell, 'Robert I and the north of England', *English Historical Review*, 73 (1958) pp389, 401.

18 Fryde, *Edward II*, p122.

19 Edward Miller, *War in the North: Anglo-Scottish Wars of Middle Ages* (St John's College Cambridge Lecture) (Hull: University of Hull, 1960), p6.

20 Fryde, *Edward II*, p122.

21 Barrow, *Robert Bruce*, pp333–34.

22 N Denholm-Young (ed), *Vita Edwardi Secundi, Monachi Cuiusdam Malmesberiensis. (The Life of Edward the Second by the so-called Monk of Malmesbury*, (London: Nelson, 1957), introduction, pxxiv. For a fuller examination of this question see N Denholm-Young, 'The authorship of the *Vita Edwardi Secundi*', *English Historical Review*, 71 (1956), pp189–211. Wendy Childs gives a largely positive opinion of Denholm-Young's conclusions in the introduction to her 2005 edition of the *Vita*, see Childs, *Vita Edwardi Secundi:*, ppxxiv–xxv.
23 Fryde, *Edward II*, chapters 4 and 5.
24 Denholm-Young, *Vita Edwardi Secundi, passim.*
25 Denholm-Young, *Vita Edwardi Secundi*, p195.

DEFENCE II
Lord Hailes' Testimony

That a promise to return the Stone of Scone was included in the Edinburgh-Northampton Treaty of 1328.

UNTIL THE EARLY NINETEENTH CENTURY the text of the Edinburgh-Northampton Treaty was unavailable and historians had to make use of other sources in order to deduce its terms. A comprehensive attempt was made by David Dalrymple (Lord Hailes) in the second volume of his *Annals of Scotland*, published in 1779. The second clause in his reconstruction reads:

The stone on which the Kings of Scotland were wont to sit at the time of their coronation shall be restored to the Scots.[1]

Towards the close of the eighteenth century an original text of the main body of the treaty was found by William Robertson in Edinburgh's Register House. His later research brought further documents to light. The findings were published in 1821.[2]

Still missing were certain other documents alluded to in the text. However, since all the actual clauses were contained in the published material, it became possible to read the terms of the treaty in full. The more important points can be summarised as follows:

i. The English Crown to acknowledge the complete independence of Scotland.
ii. King Robert's son and heir, David, to be married to King Edward's sister, Joan. (This is the same Joan mentioned in the previous chapter, but the Edward in question is now King Edward III.)
iii. If the wedding had not taken place by Michaelmas (29 September) 1338, the Scots to pay £100,000 in compensation.
iv. Scotland and England to enter into a mutual defence and assistance pact, saving only the Franco-Scottish alliance.

- v. Certain documents concerning Scotland to be returned.
- vi. The English Crown to do all it can to have the sentences of excommunication against Bruce and his subjects lifted.
- vii. King Robert to pay £20,000 to England, 'for the sake of the peace'.

At no point in the treaty is there any mention of the return of the stone at Westminster.

The only clause referring to the return of anything is v and the items in question are listed as 'writs, obligations, instruments and other muniments touching the subjection of the people or the land of Scotland to the king of England...and all other instruments and privileges touching the freedom of Scotland'.[3]

While it was just possible at the time this was written for the term 'muniment' to be stretched to include household furnishings, there is no way that the stone could have any bearing on the subjection of Scotland to the English Crown. It quite obviously lies outside the context of this clause. Furthermore, since it was identifiable, one would expect the stone to be mentioned by name. Not to do so would seem like gross carelessness on the part of the Scottish negotiators. As E L G Stones puts it:

> If an agreement had been made with the Scots at Edinburgh, it would presumably have appeared in the French indenture in company with the agreement about the return of muniments to Scotland.[4]

It is conceivable, though more than a little irregular, that an agreement concerning the return of the stone was appended to a separate document, since lost. One obvious place to begin a search for such a document would have been among the Scottish Rolls, these being the English records of business concerning Scotland.

Unfortunately, the series, as printed in the early nineteenth century, ends in January 1328, two months before the treaty was signed. The editors believed there was no roll for the second year of

Edward III's reign.[5]

In fact, there was, and it turned up during a search of the Marquess of Aylesbury's manuscripts at Savernake in 1897. It being there may or may not have something to do with the fact that one of the marquess' ancestors went by the name of Bruce – Lord Bruce of Kinloss, who just happened to be Master of the Rolls from 1603 to 1611.[6]

Among the contents of this roll is an almost complete copy of the treaty. The new items, published in 1950, consist of two notarial instruments binding Bruce to pay the £20,000 promised to England, together with letters patent promising lands worth £2,000 a year to David Bruce's intended bride Joan, this to commence the following year. With these the treaty was more or less complete and there is still no mention of the return of the stone.[7]

Misconceptions die hard and in spite of the main text having been available in printed form since the early nineteenth century, there was for a long time a tendency on the part of historians to go no further than Hailes for their information. Before the stone was returned to Scotland in 1996, the idea survived on a more popular level and seemed to have taken on the proportions of a minor legend, with attendant moral indignation, England being blamed for reneging on an agreement that was never made in the first place.[8]

It was stated above that Hailes made use of 'other sources' when making his reconstruction of the treaty. His item concerning the stone may owe something to a passage in the Chronicle of Lanercost which says:

> But the people of London would no wise allow to be taken away from them the stone of Scone, whereon the kings of Scotland used to be set at their coronations at Scone.[9]

The incident is also recorded in the chronicle of Geoffrey le Baker, though with the difference that Baker has the abbot of Westminster, rather than the people of London, refusing to hand over the stone.[10]

It would seem that there is some disagreement here between the chronicles and the text of the peace treaty. Fortunately, there is some documentary evidence available to help solve the problem:

i. A Privy Seal Writ ordering the abbot of Westminster to hand over the stone to the sheriffs of London (1 July 1328).[11]
ii. A Privy Seal writ ordering the sheriffs of London to receive the stone from the abbot and deliver it to Queen Isabella, widow of the recently-deceased Edward II (1 July 1328).[12]
iii. A letter to King Edward from John Hauteyn and Henry Darcy, the sheriffs of London, reporting that the abbot had refused to give up the stone (circa July 1328).[13]

The abbot may well have had justification for his obstinacy. When it was first brought into the abbey by Edward I, the stone was placed by the altar before the shrine of St Edward and it would seem the king intended it as an offering to the saint. There are also grounds for believing that he intended the chair in which it was enclosed to be used by the priest celebrating mass at the altar.[14]

This is not, however, to say that Edward had relinquished all rights to the stone. The wooden chair, as made by Walter the painter, included in its design two small wooden leopards, or lions, as we would say today.[15] These can be taken as a fair declaration of ownership. The arms of Edward I consist of three lions. They don't appear in those of the Confessor. There is also a record to the effect that he intended the chair to be used for coronations. All in all, we have a pretty sound basis for a dispute over ownership between the abbey and the Crown.

Although Baker's chronicle, with its view that it was the abbot who refused to hand over the stone, seems to be more in agreement with the documentary evidence, it is quite possible that the Lanercost version also contains an element of truth. A popular English song of the period declares:

> *Their kings' seat of Scone*
> *is driven over down*
> *to London led.*[16]

Judging by this, it would seem that the stone had entered into the popular consciousness and that the English populace, unconcerned with the finer points of ownership, saw it merely as a trophy of war, and something not to be given up lightly. The abbot may well have had the backing of Londoners in his refusal to give up the stone.[17]

The third of the documents outlined above also states that the decision to hand over the stone was taken by the English parliament which sat at Northampton in May 1328. It makes no reference to any agreement with the Scots. What then did Isabella want with the stone? A clue can be gleaned from a comparison of Bruce's negotiating position of October 1327 with the terms of the final treaty of the following year.

Of the six original points, all were incorporated except one. Bruce had proposed that there should be no question of anyone holding land in both Scotland and England. This does not form part of the final treaty.[18] On this point, E L G Stones says:

> We must infer that the subject of these lands was ignored by the treaty of March 1328 because after five months of negotiations the parties were not able to agree.[19]

It nevertheless seems that the disinherited English lords – particularly Henry Beaumont, Henry Percy and Thomas Wake, who claimed broad acres in Scotland – were still determined to force the issue. On 1 July, the same day as he issued the two writs outlined above, Edward III wrote to his mother authorising her to negotiate for the disinherited on both sides.[20]

The opportunity was to hand. Edward's sister Joan was to be conveyed to Berwick by 15 July for her marriage to David Bruce.[21] The couple were aged seven and four respectively. The Scots were clearly taking no chances with the £100,000 penalty clause.

Given this flurry of royal correspondence at the beginning of July, it would seem that the return of the stone and the question of the disinherited were not entirely unconnected. The plan was probably that Isabella should take the stone north, either as a bargaining counter or as a softener.[22] The obstinacy of the abbot of Westminster would appear to have spoiled this prime chance to gauge Scottish reaction to the offer. However, even without the stone, the mission still seems to have been successful.

Edward was not present at the wedding. This was taken by the Scots in the spirit it was intended and Robert the Bruce also stayed away. It was given out that he was ill though this does not seem to have prevented him from sailing to Ulster a few weeks later. We know from later references that at some point the Scots agreed to restore Percy's estates and at least a promise of restoration was made in the case of Beaumont and Wake.[23]

The occasion may well have been the royal wedding at Berwick, where Bruce's absence would serve as a partial explanation for this misguidedly generous gesture. What further concessions the Scots might have been inspired to make by the imminent prospect of getting their hands on the Westminster Stone can only remain a matter for speculation.

A final possibility which deserves some attention is that the Scots did not ask for the stone to be returned to them because their negotiating position was too weak.

Certainly there was a strong desire on the Scottish side to conclude a treaty before too much time had passed. In October 1327, when serious negotiations can be said to have begun, Robert the Bruce was 54 years old. During the summer of that year, while in Ulster, he had fallen ill to the extent that it was reported he could not survive another year. Admittedly, the report came from a hostile witness, but even so there must have been some substance underlying it.[24] The political need to place the country in a secure state before the throne passed to a minor can be seen as a strong factor in the Scottish desire for a peace treaty. To this we might couple the perfectly human desire on Bruce's part to see his life's work complete.

That said, it is possible to demonstrate an equal, perhaps even greater, need for peace on the English side by the autumn of 1327. In January of that year Edward II had been deposed by Isabella and, Mortimer, her ally and lover. Edward's son, Edward III, was crowned at Westminster on the 1 February. That very night a force of Scots crossed the Tweed and made an unsuccessful attempt to take Norham Castle on the south bank.[25]

The assault, coming on the evening of the coronation, was surely intended as a declaration that a new English king meant the start of a new chapter in relationships between the two countries. In April instructions were sent throughout England for a muster at Newcastle. The response was patchy, and rather slow. In June the main Scottish force crossed the border and burned Weardale. It was a full month after this before the main English army arrived in Durham.

In order to cut off the Scots' retreat they marched to the Tyne but the Scots failed to appear. The English army marched south again to Weardale. They found that the Scots had bypassed them and were in a strong position near Stanhope. There was a period of stalemate while the two armies faced each other across the river. A couple of nights later the Scots banked up their fires and slipped off home. For Edward there was nothing but grief. He wept with mortification.

While the army withdrew to York and began to disband, the exchequer resorted to desperate measures to meet the army's costs. Aside from general expenses there was something over £40,000 owed to mercenaries. The king's jewels were pledged towards raising the first instalment of £4,000. It would take some years and a degree of help from foreign bankers before the total cost of the campaign was met.

Within a month of the affair at Stanhope the Scots hit Northumberland again. The castles of Norham, Alnwick and Warkworth were besieged and everything not protected by stone walls was torched. Isabella and Mortimer tried to raise the army again but without much support. The end had come. In early October two English envoys came to Robert the Bruce at Norham to open negotiations for a final peace.

The terms finally agreed on were equitable. The £20,000 which the Scots agreed to pay to England was not a penalty, nor should it be seen as reparation for war damage. It is described in the treaty as being, 'for the good of the peace and for concord between the king and the king of Scotland'. In Scotland it was officially known as a 'contribution for the peace'.[26] There is no official record on either side which describes it in terms of either indemnity or compensation. To the modern eye this looks slightly puzzling. GWS Barrow has this to say:

> However unjust or illogical it may seem, it was not uncommon for one party to a dispute to pay to have its lawful rights acknowledged by the other party. The two sums offered by Bruce at different times may be seen simply as the price he was prepared to pay to silence for ever the ancient quarrel between English and Scottish kings over feudal superiority.[27]

The idea of it being reparation would also have to account for the fact that the Scots had been prepared to pay nearly £27,000 – the first of the two sums mentioned above – as early as 1323. They had done a great deal more damage since and were now about to pay less. Certainly the Scots seem to have offered this reduced sum at an early stage of the negotiations and it can in no way be seen as a concession forced out of them.[28]

As must be clear from the account above, the Scots were bargaining from a strong position. They got most of what they wanted and conceded nothing of importance. There can be little doubt that had they asked for the Westminster Stone it would have been returned to them. Since they didn't ask for it we might conclude that for some reason they just weren't interested.

Endnotes

1. David Dalrymple (Lord Hailes), *Annals of Scotland*, 3rd edition (Edinburgh: Constable, 1819), 2:158.
2. Rhymer, *Foedera, Conventiones, Litterae*, 2:2, pp734-35. A translation of excerpts from the French indenture appears in W Croft Dickinson et al (eds), *A Source Book of Scottish History*, 3 volumes (Edinburgh: Nelson, 1958), pp159-63.
3. Dickinson, *Source Book of Scottish History*, p162.
4. E L G Stones, 'An addition to the *'Rotuli Scotiae'*', *Scottish Historical Review*, 29 (1950), p33.
5. Stones, *'Rotuli Scotiae'*, p23.
6. 'Stones, *'Rotuli Scotiae'*, pp23-25.
7. On items still missing see Stones, *'Rotuli Scotiae'*, p29.
8. Some historians who followed Hailes are named in E L G Stones, 'The Treaty of Northampton, 1328', *History*, 38, (1953), pp54-61.
9. H Maxwell, *Chronicle of Lanercost*, p260.
10. Rodwell, *Coronation Chair*, p17.
11. J Strachey (ed), *Rotuli Parliamentorum*, Volume 2 (London, 1767-1777), p442.
12. A H Thomas (ed), *Calendar of Plea and Memorandum Rolls of the City of London*, &c, Volume 1 (1323-1364), (1926), 1 July 1328.
13. *Calendar of Plea and Memorandum Rolls of the City of London*, No date: circa July 1328.
14. Rodwell, *Coronation Chair*, pp17, 21.
15. Rodwell, *Coronation Chair*, p36.
16. G W S Barrow, *Robert Bruce and the Community of the Realm of Scotland*, 4th edition (Edinburgh, 2005), p96.
17. 'La Piere D'Escoce', p112. The two chronicles are confused towards the foot of the page.
18. *Robert Bruce*, pp331-32, 336-39.
19. Stones, 'The Anglo-Scottish negotiations of 1327', p52.
20. Stones, *'Rotuli Scotiae'*, pp33-35, 50-51.
21. Stones, *Anglo-Scottish Relations*, 41, pp165-66.
22. *'Rotuli Scotiae'*, pp34-35.

23 Stones, *'Rotuli Scotiae'*, p35; Stones, *Anglo-Scottish Relations,* 42, pp171–72; Ranald Nicholson, *Edward III and the Scots: the formative years of a military career* (London: Oxford University Press, 1965), pp57–59.
24 Barrow, *Robert Bruce*, p328.
25 For the Weardale campaign of 1327, see Barrow, *Robert Bruce*, pp328–30 and Nicholson, *Edward III*, chapters 2 and 3.
26 Stones, *'Rotuli Scotiae'*, p29 and n2.
27 Barrow, *Robert Bruce*, p338, Stones, *'Rotuli Scotiae'*, pxxx.
28 Stones, 'The Anglo-Scottish negotiations of 1327', pp49–54.

THE INVESTIGATION

IF THE BALANCE of evidence presented suggests that some sort of substitution of stones may have taken place, the obvious thing now would be to try to discover who might have been responsible.

The Time Limits

Edward I crossed the Tweed into Scotland on 28 March 1296. A month later, almost to the day, the last serious Scottish resistance ended with the defeat of Balliol's army at Dunbar. It would seem fairly safe to assume then that the stone was not moved before the end of April. Nobody before that time could have predicted either the speed or the extent of the Scottish collapse. What they might have predicted was that Edward would take steps to secure the north of the country, which meant passing through Perth.

The English king arrived there on Thursday, 21 June and stayed until the following Monday. All the contemporary sources agree that the stone which went to London was taken, not at this time but later, in August, when the king passed through the town again after an extensive tour of the north.[1]

Anyone bent on removing the original stone, however, could not simply assume that Edward, who had shown considerable energy in the course of his three-day stay in Perth, would not ride out the short distance to Scone or visit it on his way north. This was after all the ancient capital of the kingdom he had just conquered and the stone was the enthronement seat of kings whose position and privileges he had just taken for himself.

So we can say with some confidence that the alleged deed must have been done at some time during the period of almost eight weeks between the surrender at Dunbar on 28 April and Edward's arrival in Perth on 21 June.

The Suspects

Establishing a list of suspects for an incident which took place over seven centuries ago is not the simplest of tasks. The only thing we can be fairly sure of is that whoever did it must have been a person of some position in the kingdom. One would not expect to roll up at the ancient capital and remove an ancient relic without the necessary authority, either legal or physical.

We must grant that whoever took the stone either had the judicial power to do so or came with enough force as to render protest ineffectual, or perhaps both. The person in question would almost certainly be a member of one of these groups:

> The earls [...] By 1296, the seven divisions of ancient Alba had evolved, through division and the addition of two from the south of the Forth, into fourteen earldoms. One of these – Gowrie – was in Crown hands.[2]
>
> The barons [...] There were many. We might consider those whose lands were so extensive as to set them head and shoulders above the rest. These were Alexander MacDougall, lord of Argyll and Lorne, and John Comyn the elder, lord of Badenoch and Lochaber [Known as the Black Comyn, he was father of John the Red Comyn, who had been taken prisoner at Dunbar.] The other great lordship, Galloway, was held by John Balliol, king of Scots.
>
> The bishops [...] In the absence of a primate, the bishops of Scotland were in theory all equal. However, two of them, the bishops of St Andrews and Glasgow, were decidedly more equal than the others. The sheer size and location of their dioceses was enough to determine this. The bishopric of Glasgow ran from Teviotdale to the head of Loch Lomond while that of St Andrews swept round in an extensive arc covering most of the eastern side of the country from the Tweed to the Dee. Along Tayside it stretched as far west as Scone.[3]

Beside these, there are three individuals who ought to be considered:

The king of Scots.
The justiciar of Scotland north of the Forth
...and the abbot of Scone.

We are thus looking at a list of twenty men:

John Balliol, king of Scots.
Gilbert de Umfraville, earl of Angus.
John of Strathbogie, earl of Atholl.
John Comyn, earl of Buchan.
John, earl of Caithness.
Robert Bruce, earl of Carrick.
Patrick Dunbar, earl of Dunbar or March.
Duncan MacDuff, earl of Fife.[4]
Malcolm, earl of Lennox.
Donald, earl of Mar.
Alexander Menteith, earl of Menteith.
William, earl of Ross.
Malise, earl of Strathearn.
William Sutherland, earl of Sutherland.
Alexander MacDougall, lord of Argyll.
John Comyn, lord of Badenoch and Lochaber.
William Fraser, bishop of St Andrews.
Robert Wishart, bishop of Glasgow.
Thomas, abbot of Scone.
Andrew Murray, justiciar of Scotia, i.e. Scotland north of the Forth.

We can start by getting rid of those with watertight alibis.

Excluded by Alibi

William Fraser, bishop of St Andrews, was the senior of the four ambassadors who negotiated the alliance between John Balliol and the French king, Philip the Fair. He left Scotland in 1295 and died in France in 1297.[5]

William, earl of Ross, was one of the Scottish earls who occupied Dunbar Castle in the spring of 1296. Ross was taken prisoner there when it surrendered on 28 April. He was sent to the Tower of London and not released until 1303. Later, he was to distinguish himself as the man who delivered Bruce's wife and daughter into the hands of the English.[6]

John of Strathbogie, earl of Atholl, accompanied the earl of Ross to Dunbar and to the Tower. However, he was released earlier, on 30 July 1297, having agreed to serve with the English army in Flanders.[7]

Andrew Murray, justiciar of Scotia, was captured at Dunbar, sent to the Tower of London and held there until at least the close of the following year.[8]

Duncan MacDuff, earl of Fife, was still a child in 1296. Presumably he stayed at home.[9]

John, earl of Caithness, swore fealty by proxy at Murkle on the shores of the Pentland Firth in August 1296. This would seem to have been taken as an adequate substitute for his coming to Berwick because on 28 August, the date of the Ragman Roll, he was granted protection for one year following Michaelmas. There is no reason to suggest he ever left his own country and, considering he was probably as much Norwegian as Scottish, no reason to suspect he might have wanted to.[10]

With those discounted, our list now looks like this:

John Balliol, king of Scots.
Gilbert de Umfraville, earl of Angus.
John Comyn, earl of Buchan.
Robert Bruce, earl of Carrick.
Patrick Dunbar, earl of Dunbar or March.
Malcolm, earl of Lennox.
Donald, earl of Mar.
Alexander Menteith, earl of Menteith.
Malise, earl of Strathearn.
William Sutherland, earl of Sutherland.
Alexander MacDougall, lord of Argyll.
John Comyn, lord of Badenoch and Lochaber.

Robert Wishart, bishop of Glasgow.
Thomas, abbot of Scone.

There are fourteen men left, any one of whom might have been at the scene of the alleged incident at the time in question. The next thing to examine is motive. We can start by looking at those who are highly unlikely to have had any.

Excluded by Lack of Motive

Alexander Menteith, earl of Menteith, was with the earls of Atholl and Ross during the spring campaign and, like them, was captured at Dunbar. However, he seems to have either enjoyed some special favour with Edward or to have been more convincing in his renunciation of his evil ways because he was released from prison 'by the king's grace' and his earldom was restored to him.

He swore fealty to Edward at Elgin on 27 July and again on the Ragman Roll at Berwick in August. It seems quite likely that he accompanied the king on his royal progress through the country.[11]

Malcolm, earl of Lennox, is said by Walter of Guisborough to have been one of the seven earls of Scotland who crossed the border and raided into England that spring.[12] This seems rather inconsistent with some other aspects of his behaviour at the time. The Scottish army was ordered to muster at Caddonlee – near Selkirk, where the Caddon Water meets the Tweed – on 11 March.[13] Lennox swore fealty to Edward three days later.[14]

This, taking place a clear two weeks before Edward crossed the border, seems a rather eccentric act for a man about to take up arms against him. Lennox, however, was a very cautious man. Eighteen months later at Stirling Bridge he acted as mediator between the earl of Surrey and William Wallace. When his services were no longer required he hung around the neighbouring wood and, when the English ranks broke, swooped on their fleeing baggage train.[15] All in all, it is difficult to imagine this man securing a national relic unless he could see a ready market for it.

William Sutherland, earl of Sutherland, was a man of around 60 at the time. His name appears on the Ragman Roll though in his case his fealty may have been taken by proxy. If this is true we can assume he stayed in his own country. Considering its remoteness and his advanced years this would seem a sensible course of action. He remained faithful to England until his death about ten years later.[16]

Aside from these three there were others who, far from being uninterested, were actively engaged on the English side. Their motive, if any, would have been to ensure that Edward gained possession of a guaranteed genuine stone.

Patrick Dunbar, earl of Dunbar or March, left his castle at Dunbar in the hands of his wife in order to join Edward at Berwick. In 1298 he was appointed captain of the English garrison at Berwick and later commander of the English forces of the East March.[17]

Gilbert de Umfraville, earl of Angus, was an Englishman. His father had gained the Angus earldom through marriage. The de Umfravilles were a Northumberland family, lords of Coquetdale and Redesdale, both of which were burned by the Scots in April. Gilbert was with Edward at the Battle of Falkirk in 1298. He remained in the English interest until his death in 1307. His son fought for Edward's son at Bannockburn.[18]

Robert Bruce, earl of Carrick, in company with his father, who had handed over the earldom in 1292, held Carlisle Castle for Edward against the Scots. He later crossed the Solway into Annandale at the head of an English force. Along with the earls of Angus and Dunbar he had renewed his fealty to Edward at his camp at Wark, just south of the Tweed, on 26 March. Ten years later, in 1306, he was crowned king of Scots at Scone.[19]

Donald, earl of Mar, was not actively engaged on the English side but might be counted as a sympathiser. There was a family link with Robert the Bruce through Bruce's fairly recent marriage to his daughter, Isabel. Mar seems to have attended Edward during the king's journey round Scotland in 1291. In early August 1296, while travelling south from Elgin, Edward spent two nights as Mar's guest at Kildrummy Castle.

Yet we are asked to believe, by Guisborough, that Donald of Mar was one of the seven earls who ravaged the north of England earlier in the year. Considering this would have involved besieging his own son-in-law in Carlisle, and, bearing in mind that the earl of Lennox, also said to be one of their number, had sworn fealty to Edward three days *after* the muster at Caddonlee, it might perhaps pay us to look at this question a little more closely.[20]

The Seven Earls of Scotland

A twelfth-century description of Scotland, going under the title of *De Situ Albanie*, which is itself a composite of earlier accounts, relates how the country north of the Forth was divided into seven parts. It talks of these being ruled by seven under-kings.[21]

As said above, by the late thirteenth century, there were actually fourteen earldoms. However, due to a revival of interest in the Celtic past at the time, the concept if not the substance of the seven earls was still very much alive.[22] Guisborough names Buchan, Menteith, Strathearn, Lennox, Ross, Atholl and Mar, together with John Comyn the younger of Badenoch, as being the leaders of a Scottish force that burst out of Annandale on Easter Monday and burned villages all the way to Carlisle. On the Wednesday, after an abortive siege of the city, they returned to Annandale.[23] They next met at Jedburgh on Sunday, 8 April and moved into England through Redesdale. After a diversion to besiege Harbottle Castle for two days before giving up on it, there followed fire and slaughter down to the Tyne Valley, passing through Corbridge and on to burn Hexham with its abbey, then further west to burn the nunnery of Lambley. Thursday night found them at Lanercost Priory. According to Guisborough, the Scots were informed that a body of English troops was nearby and so the following morning they took the road home.[24]

A different view of events is given in the chronicle which is generally believed to come from Lanercost Priory. This account tells of a two-pronged attack, with Buchan striking at Cumberland while another force moved through Redesdale and on to destroy Hexham, Lambley and Lanercost.

On their return – there is no mention of an English force – this second contingent is said to have split into two, one part occupying the passes bordering on Teviotdale, the other 'the narrow pass into Lothian'[25]

Lanercost Priory

– this is probably Soutra, which cuts between the Lammermuir and Moorfoot Hills. Both detachments were well placed to threaten the flank of the English forces when they moved north from Berwick.

When the Guisborough account is plotted on a map it becomes clear that this obsession with the idea of seven earls as an inseparable band of brothers involves the Scottish forces in a great deal of extra mileage. Moving out of Cumberland to go back to Annandale, then up to Jedburgh – around 45 miles as the crow flies but further on foot or horseback – in order to strike at Cumberland again *from the east* seems to imply at the very least a fairly *ad hoc* approach to planning.

All in all, the Lanercost version, written at the scene of the action, seems more in accordance with the realities of the time, with just Buchan leading the attack on Cumberland. Considering the fierce independence of the people of Galloway, this would have made for a sensible division of labour. Buchan was in a sense a local man, being lord of Cruggleton, in Wigtownshire, and sheriff of the county.[26]

The other Scottish leaders could then have left the Galloway men to the business they well understood, while moving their forces into England by the more familiar Redesdale route. Whether or not

Ross, Atholl and Menteith led the Redesdale raid is irrelevant. The records clearly point to their later presence at Dunbar.

It was about this time, according to Guisborough, that Earl Patrick left his castle at Dunbar in the hands of his wife, Marjory, in order to be with his king at Berwick. It's worth mentioning here that Marjory was sister of the earl of Buchan.[27] Guisborough has her sending a messenger to the Scottish forces and inveigling them into the castle past her husband's garrison.[28] Lanercost says that she defended it for two days before being persuaded that her husband was a traitor.[29]

The two versions are not incompatible and, whatever the details, the castle was in Scottish hands by 23 April – St George's Day.[30] At this point Guisborough breaks with his pattern, mentioning only the earls of Ross, Atholl and Menteith.[31]

Two days later, after the main Scottish army had been defeated outside Dunbar, the castle surrendered. The English list of prisoners taken there is headed by the three earls of Ross, Atholl and Menteith.[32] It is rather curious that at the point where English official documentation makes contact with Scottish military activity, Guisborough should suddenly discard four of his seven earls.

They do not show up anywhere else. There is nothing to equate with the Lanercost account of a division of forces on the way home from Redesdale. Neither are they said to have joined up with the main Scottish army which advanced on Dunbar. The only man to be mentioned by name is Sir Patrick Graham, who, when the Scottish advance went into reverse, stood his ground and died on the battlefield.[33] It may be significant that, although casualties were said to be heavy, there were no other men of rank among the dead. If Lennox, Mar and Strathearn were there, they presumably led from a discreet distance and made themselves scarce at an early stage in the proceedings.

However, we only have Guisborough's word for these three earls being active in any part of the conflict. In the light of what has been said above, it would seem reasonable to conclude that the chronicler, or his source, has allowed a notion of romantic chivalry or Celtic revivalism to obscure the facts of the matter.

Given what we know of the character and general behaviour

of Lennox and Mar, it seems likely that the Lanercost version is closer to the truth, and that these two at least were not actively involved. We can return to Malise of Strathearn later. Meanwhile, we can probably discount the possibility of Lennox and Mar being sufficiently motivated to move stones.

Without these two, and the other men mentioned above, our list reads:

>   John Balliol, king of Scots.
>   John Comyn, earl of Buchan.
>   Malise, earl of Strathearn.
>   Alexander MacDougall, lord of Argyll.
>   John Comyn, lord of Badenoch and Lochaber.
>   Robert Wishart, bishop of Glasgow.
>   Thomas, abbot of Scone.

Debarred by Later Events

Thomas, abbot of Scone swore fealty to Edward at Perth on 24 July 1291 and we find his name on the Ragman Roll, dated 28 August 1296.[34] These fealties cannot be taken to indicate any particular attitude on his part since on both occasions almost all those of any position in Scotland were doing likewise. What they do indicate, quite obviously, is that he was abbot of Scone during the spring of 1296, and if any person or persons unknown did remove a certain item of furniture, it was almost certainly with his knowledge, and quite possibly with his collusion.

He may have lived to regret the fact. His name is on the document which records the destruction of the abbey by Edward's men after Falkirk.[35] This is dated 17 August 1298. It is possibly through the abbot's initiative in providing some sort of substitute that the English king's wrath was stayed for two years.

After this there seems to have been something of a power struggle in Scone. As the introduction to the 1843 edition of the *Liber Ecclesie de Scon* puts it, 'The English party in the convent, or perhaps Edward by his sovereign authority, had, in the meantime, chosen another abbot'.[36] This was Henry and he seems to have been in post at the time of Bruce's coronation in March 1306.

When Bruce was inaugurated as king of Scots, every effort seems to have been made to do things in the proper manner, with due respect for tradition.[37] Thomas may or may not have been physically present but if he had information to impart concerning the whereabouts of the traditional central prop, this would have been no time to keep a still tongue. We know he was still alive because he was abbot again in 1312.[38] Back in 1296 he had been custodian of the stone. If he took it upon himself to hide it, the knowledge of its location would have become as precious as the relic itself and he would have been under every obligation, moral and legal, to pass this knowledge on. Simply to omit to do so would seem both irrational and unreasonable.

There is of course a more practical aspect. The idea of an abbot barrowing what we might expect to have been a sizeable lump of masonry, presumably by moonlight and alone, involves us in attributing to him not only considerable physical strength but also a scant regard for dignity and a severe deficiency of common sense.

Others, most likely some of the monks, must have been involved and thus, even if Thomas did leave a certain tale untold, there would have been those in a position to pass on the information. It is hard to accept that nobody would have had the initiative to croak out the details before dying, and that within ten years all knowledge of the location had been lost by the inhabitants of Scone Abbey.

In the face of this, the most plausible conclusion has to be that Thomas didn't know, that no one in the abbey knew, and that we have to delete him from our list of suspects.

Robert Wishart, bishop of Glasgow, presents us with a similar problem. A consistent enemy of the English crown, of all the men on the list he was the one who seems to have suffered most in the cause of Robert the Bruce. He was one of the prime movers of the revolt of 1297, which led to the Scottish victory at Stirling Bridge and to the later defeat at Falkirk. When in 1306 Bruce knifed John Comyn the younger (the Red Comyn) at the high altar of the Greyfriars' church in Dumfries, Wishart could have excommunicated him. Instead he urged his flock to take up arms in Bruce's support.

He was present at the coronation at Scone six weeks later and was active in the revolt which followed. Using timber which the English had given him to repair the bell tower of his cathedral, he constructed siege-engines for an assault on the castle at Kirkintilloch. He himself fell on the castle at Cupar 'like a warrior'.[39] It was a considerable burst of activity for a bishop of advanced years.

The rest of his life was to be somewhat quieter. Captured at Cupar soon afterwards, he was sent as a prisoner into England. On hearing the news, Edward wrote to Aymer de Valence, his lieutenant in Scotland, saying that he was as pleased by Wishart's capture as he would have been by that of Bruce himself. The bishop was to be placed in irons and treated without regard for his status as a priest.

While others were set free, Wishart remained a prisoner into the reign of Edward II. It took the victory at Bannockburn to bring about his release. When he finally returned to Scotland, in company with Bruce's wife, sister and daughter, he was very old, and blind.[40]

We have here a man whose motive for securing the stone would have been of the highest order. We must allow him the opportunity. He swore fealty to Edward on 26 July 1296 at Elgin and there is no record of his whereabouts prior to this date.[41] He could equally have been at Scone as anywhere else.

There is even evidence to suggest that, for Wishart, safeguarding the stone would have been very much in character. When he met with Bruce after the Comyn murder, Wishart supplied him with robes and vestments suitable for his coronation. He also produced a banner bearing the arms of the last king. This he had kept carefully hidden away for ten years. G W S Barrow has this to say:

> It was a picturesque touch, and reminds us forcefully that the mind of Wishart had most probably been behind the drafting of the Treaty of Birgham, which sixteen years earlier had provided so elaborately that relics and muniments touching the royal dignity should be kept safely, under their seals, by the great magnates of the realm.[42]

In all of Scotland, there was no object which so closely touched the royal dignity as the Stone of Scone. And yet when Bruce was crowned, Wishart could not produce the stone. It has to be stressed again that great care was taken to give the ceremony, which was by way of being the endorsement of a military coup, all semblance of legality and propriety. It was performed on Friday, 25 March. The earl of Fife, whose ancient right it was to enthrone the new king, was absent, a ward of Edward in England. His sister Isabel, the countess of Buchan, stole her husband's horses and rode to Scone. She arrived too late for the ceremony so a second one was staged two days later, purely in order that a representative of the MacDuffs should fulfil the family role.[43]

Given this almost obsessive attention to detail, we have to conclude that if Wishart could not deliver the stone, he never had it in the first place. And given that neither he nor the abbot of Scone took the elementary step of securing it, the most likely explanation would seem to be that someone else got there first, and furthermore that the somebody else was a person or persons who, ten years later, would have been totally opposed to the enthronement of Robert the Bruce.

We are left with five names, men who we might call:

The Accused

John Balliol, king of Scots.
John Comyn, earl of Buchan.
Malise, earl of Strathearn.
Alexander MacDougall, lord of Argyll.
John Comyn, lord of Badenoch and Lochaber.

They become rather more of a unit if we look at this tree:

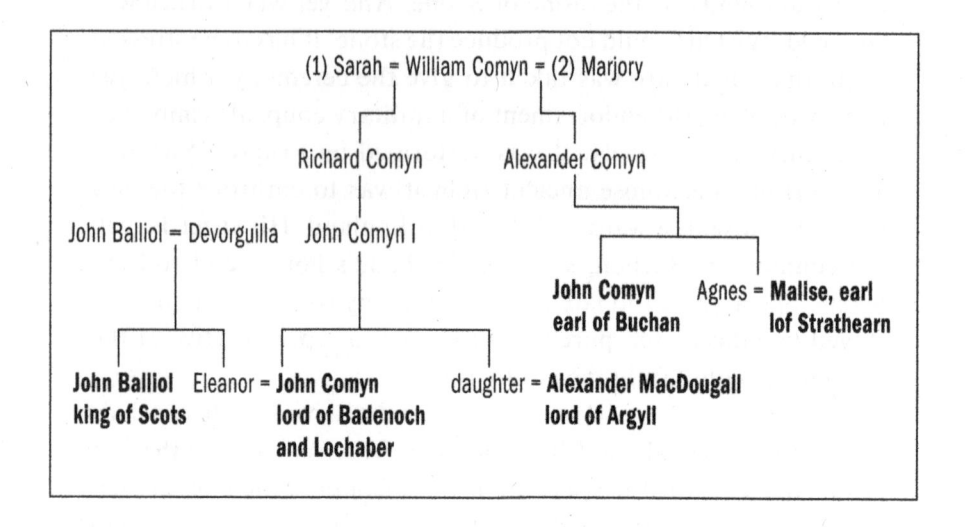

```
                    (1) Sarah = William Comyn = (2) Marjory
                          |                        |
                    Richard Comyn            Alexander Comyn
                          |                        |
John Balliol = Devorguilla   John Comyn I          |
        |                          |         John Comyn      Agnes = Malise, earl
        |                          |         earl of Buchan         lof Strathearn
John Balliol   Eleanor = John Comyn      daughter = Alexander MacDougall
king of Scots          lord of Badenoch            lord of Argyll
                       and Lochaber
```

Besides the ties of blood and marriage shown above there was one more. All of them were totally opposed to any claim to the throne put forward by a member of the Bruce family.

We can say that any one of them could have done it. This, however, hardly constitutes proof of guilt. In fact, there are certain aspects of the character and behaviour of three of them which make it rather difficult to believe that they might have been involved.

Malise, earl of Strathearn, submitted to Edward on 19 June when the king was at Stirling.[44] It is possible within the constraints of time that the whole business was settled before then. However, the idea of Malise being caught up in such a weighty matter as this, then rushing south to become one of the very first of his country to submit after Dunbar, lacks consistency. Perhaps we should return a 'not proven' verdict in terms at least of his involvement in the latter part of the business.

Alexander MacDougall, lord of Argyll and Lorne's position is more complex in that he submitted to Edward at Elgin on 26 July, this being two weeks after Badenoch and Buchan submitted at Montrose and long after the time when the stone might have been moved.[45] The problem with Alexander is that we do not know where he was before this. He may have been with the Scottish forces in the south – though there is no mention of his name – or he may have come direct from his own country. The whole business could well have been over and done with a month before he stirred himself. If he was involved we have to assume that he detached himself from the others in order to surrender alone at a later date.

It seems more likely that Alexander came to Elgin because it was, after Perth, the easiest point on Edward's tour to reach from his castle at Dunstaffnage, that his journey was more or less direct and that prior to this he had been at home. With this in mind it would seem best to declare him 'innocent' of the charge.

John Balliol, king of Scots. There is very little in this man's character to indicate that he might have carried out such a deed on his own initiative, and even less to recommend him as a participant in someone else's venture. That he was a walking security risk must have been apparent even before his abject and complete capitulation later in the summer. His tendency towards bluster followed by total collapse had already been demonstrated in front of the English parliament three years before. Mistrust of him had grown to such an extent that the government of the country was formally taken out of his hands at the Stirling parliament of 1295.[46]

To declare him 'innocent' is perhaps to pay him a compliment. There remain two men, both with the same name:

John Comyn the elder, lord of Badenoch and Lochaber, Guardian of Scotland.

John Comyn, earl of Buchan, Constable of Scotland.

Endnotes

1. Rothwell, *Walter of Guisborough*, p281; Thomas Hog (ed), *F Nicholai Triveti, Annales sex regum Angliae... 1136-1307*, (London: English Historical Society, 1845), p349; repeated in Riley, *Willelmi Rishanger*, p163.
2. G W S Barrow, *The Kingdom of the Scots* (Edinburgh University Press, 2003), pp269-70.
3. The dioceses are mapped in Peter McNeill and Ranald Nicholson, *An Historical Atlas of Scotland*, (St Andrews, 1975), pp136, 138-9. On the ecclesiastical organisation of Scotland at the time see pp35-36. The position of the Scottish bishops is considered in G W S. Barrow, 'The Scottish Clergy in the War of Independence', *Scottish Historical Review*, 41 (1962). This also appears as chapter 10 of Barrow, *Kingdom*.
4. On the use of family names, see James Balfour Paul, *The Scots Peerage*, (Edinburgh: Constable, 9 volumes, 1904-1914). On the status of the name MacDuff, see Barrow, *Robert Bruce*, pp76-77.
5. Barrow, *Kingdom*, p217.
6. Maxwell, *Chronicle of Lanercost*, p 176; Rothwell, *Walter of Guisborough*, p279; Bain, *Calendar of Documents*, 2:742, 1395, 1399; John Barbour, *The Bruce* (Edinburgh: Canongate, 2009), p152; F J H and W F Skene, *John of Fordun's Chronicle of the Scottish Nation* (Edinburgh, 1872), 1:342; 2:334-5.
7. Bain, *Calendar of Documents*, 2:742, 930, 940, 942.
8. Bain, *Calendar of Documents*, 2:742, 960. On the position and role of the justiciars see Barrow, *Kingdom*, chapter 3.
9. Paul, *The Scots Peerage*, 4:11.
10. Bain, *Calendar of Documents*, 2:803, 839.
11. Bain, *Calendar of Documents*, 2:742, 823.
12. Rothwell, *Walter of Guisborough*, pp272-73.
13. Barrow, *Robert Bruce*, pp87-88.
14. Bain, *Calendar of Documents*, 2:730.
15. Barrow, *Robert Bruce*, pp114-15. By contrast, his son became one of Robert the Bruce's most devoted followers during the fugitive period after the Battle of Methven. Following the new king's second defeat at Dail Righ, near Tyndrum, at the hands of John MacDougall it was through the Lennox country that Bruce made his escape to Bute and Rathlin. It is questionable whether Bruce would have survived had it

not been for the loyal support of the earl and his people. The younger Lennox remained faithful until the king's death, outliving him to die in changed times amidst the carnage of Halidon Hill. The idea that the earl who was at Stirling Bridge was the same man who later followed Bruce, rather than them being father and son, seems to stem solely from an undated charter. Against this we have to set the letter written by Margaret, Countess of Lennox, to Edward in 1303 asking for his help against Comyn of Badenoch, As suggested in Paul, *The Scots Peerage*, the fact that she wrote in her own name would seem to indicate that she was a widow at the time. There is also some discrepancy between the conduct of the earl in 1297 and the earl of 1306. The actions of Lennox after Bruce's coronation seem to speak rather of a young man new to his position rather than one who had been earl for about 35 years. See Paul, *The Scots Peerage*, 5:333–6, especially 334.

16 Bain, *Calendar of Documents*, 2:823; Paul, *The Scots Peerage*, 8:323. On the question of personal attendance at Berwick to swear fealty, see Barrow, *Robert Bruce*, pp100–2.

17 Paul, *The Scots Peerage*, 3:262-3; Rothwell, *Walter of Guisborough*, p277; Bain, *Calendar of Documents*, 2:1023, 1025. Patrick, along with the earl of Angus and the two Bruces, swore fealty at Wark on 25 March, three days before Edward crossed the Tweed. Rothwell, *Walter of Guisborough*, pp283–4; Stones, *Anglo-Scottish Relations*, 22.

18 Barrow, *Robert Bruce*, pp132, 301, 354–55; Paul, *The Scots Peerage*, 1:167–8.

19 Bain, *Calendar of Documents*, 2:716, 950; Rothwell, *Walter of Guisborough*, pp283–4; Stones, *Anglo-Scottish Relations*, 22.

20 Paul, *The Scots Peerage*, 5:577–8; Rothwell, *Walter of Guisborough*, pp272–73. See also Stevenson, *Documents Illustrative of the History of Scotland*, 2:352.

21 Dickinson, *Source Book of Scottish History*, 1:4.

22 Barrow, *Robert Bruce*, pp58-60.

23 Rothwell, *Walter of Guisborough*, pp272–74.

24 Rothwell, *Walter of Guisborough*, pp276–77.

25 Maxwell, *Chronicle of Lanercost*, pp135–36, 138.

26 Barrow, *Robert Bruce*, p145.

27 Paul, *The Scots Peerage* 3:263–4.

28 Rothwell, *Walter of Guisborough*, p277.

29 Maxwell, *Chronicle of Lanercost*, p138.

30   An account of the campaign together with Edward's subsequent tour of Scotland, in the form of an itinerary written in French, appears in Stevenson, *Documents Illustrative of the History of Scotland*, 2:352, translated in Dickinson, *Source Book of Scottish History*, 1:7-10. Obviously the product of someone in the English camp, its chronological accuracy is borne out by the dates and places of origin of the king's writs.

31   Rothwell, *Walter of Guisborough*, p279.

32   Bain, *Calendar of Documents*, 2:742.

33   Rothwell, *Walter of Guisborough*, p278.

34   Bain, *Calendar of Documents*, 2:508, 823.

35   *Liber Ecclesie de Scon*, 124. See also xi.

36   *Liber Ecclesie de Scon*, xii.

37   Barrow, *Robert Bruce*, p196.

38   *Liber Ecclesie de Scon*, 104:144.

39   *Liber Ecclesie de Scon*, 104:197 and *passim*.

40   Barbour, *The Bruce*, p516; Bain, *Calendar of Documents*, 3:393.

41   Bain, *Calendar of Documents*, 2:823.

42   Barrow, *Robert Bruce*, p193. The treaty is printed in Stevenson, *Documents Illustrative of the History of Scotland*, 1:108. There is a translation of excerpts in Dickinson, *Source Book of Scottish History*, 1:123–5.

43   Barrow, *Robert Bruce*, p193.

44   Bain, *Calendar of Documents*, 2:823; also Stevenson, *Documents Illustrative of the History of Scotland*, 2:352.

45   Bain, *Calendar of Documents*, 2:791. His signature also appears on the Ragman Roll. Bain, *Calendar of Documents*, 2:823. However, on 10 September, the earl of Menteith was empowered to take over his castles, isles and lands. Whatever this says about Alexander of Argyll, it surely counts as another sign of Edward's partiality towards Alexander of Menteith, Whether Menteith managed to carry out his commission is another matter. Bain, *Calendar of Documents*, 2:823.

46   Barrow, *Robert Bruce*, pp78, 83.

THE HEIST

WE NEED TO BE WARY of hindsight. The following year, William Wallace and Andrew Murray – the son of the justiciar of the same name – led a peasant army against the mailed chivalry of England at Stirling Bridge, and won. The shock was considerable, such a thing almost unheard of. To drive the message home, Wallace led his men into the north of England, bringing down on it all the horrors attendant on the visit of an undisciplined bloodthirsty horde.

Between this invasion and the Battle of Bannockburn, Scotland was invaded five times and horror became commonplace.

In 1306 Bruce stabbed his chief rival, John Comyn the younger, over a church altar in Dumfries and had himself made king. Two years later, he went through the Comyn country of Buchan with fire and sword, wasting it to such an extent that, according to Barbour, men grieved for 50 years.[1]

In 1314, on the carse of the Forth, near Stirling, a more experienced but still largely peasant army triumphed once more over heavy armour, and the king of England was chased over the border.

Back in 1296 such things could not be foreseen, either in dreams or in nightmares. After the Scottish defeat at Dunbar, the war was virtually over. The rules of the time did not encourage anything as crude as total war, and nobody had given the signal to start breaking the rules.[2] Edinburgh Castle held out for a while, an act of largely passive resistance. At Stirling only the porter stayed behind to hand over the keys and not even pride was saved. For those Scots who remained free, there was little to decide except where and when to submit.

However, there was still one uncertainty, one thing which could not be predicted, this being how Edward would treat King John, and consequently, what arrangements would be made for the future government of Scotland. Various alternatives might have occupied the minds of the Scottish leaders who were still at large that spring, one possibility being what did in fact happen, that John would be stripped of his kingdom and sent into exile and Scotland put under military rule.

An alternative might have been the setting up of a puppet king. There would have been little difficulty in finding a candidate. It was only five years since thirteen men – including John Comyn the elder of Badenoch – had stepped forward and claimed a right to the Scottish throne. In fact, after Dunbar, Robert Bruce – the son of the unsuccessful and now dead Bruce the Competitor and the father of the future king – put forward his own plea for the throne. Edward's reply was the rather scathing, 'Have we nothing else to do but win kingdoms for you?'[3] However, it is unlikely that such a clear-cut indication of Edward's attitude would have come through to men on the run and, even so, it might not have extended to all possible candidates.

It is also conceivable that the Comyns might have had ideas of their own. Considering his record, they may well have been feeling rather jaundiced towards John Balliol by this time. The previous year at Stirling, the government had been formally taken out of his hands and entrusted to an elected council of twelve – which included Badenoch, Buchan and Strathearn.[4]

This, together with the sight of the kingdom in collapse, might possibly have inclined them towards the idea of Balliol's abdication in favour of his son, Edward. This younger Balliol had been described as the future king of Scotland in the French treaty of 1295.[5] By the spring of 1296 that future could have been seen as a distinct improvement on the current state of affairs.

We can speculate endlessly on the various possibilities, as no doubt the Comyns did. There is one thing, however, which they would have been only too well aware of. Four years before, when John Balliol assumed the title of king of Scots, it had been by enthronement on the Stone of Scone. In the course of the ceremony, a crown had been placed on his head, but this was incidental. Being placed on the stone meant the assumption of kingship.[6]

The ritual is essentially, though not exclusively, Celtic, and there are numerous recorded examples of such stones designed either for enthronement, as at Scone, or incorporating an appropriately shaped depression in which the new leader would place his foot. At Dunadd in Argyll, the Dalriadic kings may have assumed office by placing their right foot in what was said to be the footprint of Fergus Mor mac Erc, the first of their line to rule in Scotland. Kings of Ireland took office by standing on the Lia Fal. According to legend the stone would sound under genuine kings but remain silent under the feet of a usurper.[7]

At Scone, kings were enthroned by the head of the MacDuff family, the earl of Fife. This privilege went back to the twelfth century, when the mormaers, later the earls, of Fife were acknowledged as the senior nobility. In 1292 the then earl was an infant and the job of enthroning Balliol was formally entrusted to the Englishman, Sir John de St John.[8] Bishop Bek of Durham was also in attendance. It has been argued that these two, present as witnesses, might have noticed a disparity between the stone used at Balliol's enthronement and the one which went south four years later.[9] However, if we go back to the previous king's enthronement, that of Alexander III in 1249, which was described in more detail by the chronicler John of Fordun, we hear that the stone was 'decked with silken cloths inwoven with gold'.[10] This is no less than would have been expected for Balliol. (Given that his enthronement took place on 30 November he might also have expected a cushion or two.) Barrow states that Guisborough's account of John's inauguration presumably comes from an eyewitness.[11] It isn't unlikely that Sir John and the bishop, being there in an official capacity, would have had less opportunity to observe details of the stone in undress than the monk or member of the Bruce family who most likely supplied the description.

Fourteen years later, when Bruce made his bid for the throne the earl was a ward of King Edward. His sister, Isabel, took his place and a gold coronet was placed on Bruce's head.[12] Under the circumstances, it was the best that could be done, but it would have been better if it had been done, according to custom and practice, on the stone.

The idea of Bruce becoming king of Scots can hardly have been in the mind of the Comyns in 1296. He was, after all, busily engaged in the service of the English Crown at the time. However, they should have been aware of the possibility of a new king in the not-too-distant future. Presumably they would also have believed, as men of their time, that a new king, whether set up by English or Comyn power, could only have been properly inaugurated by enthronement on the Stone of Scone.

To this must be added the previously mentioned obligation embodied in the Treaty of Birgham – which Badenoch had helped to negotiate – for 'the greatest of the realm' to keep safely all relics touching the royal dignity. Given that these two men comprised most of the power in the north, that they were at large at the time and almost overburdened with motive, means and opportunity, it would be approaching the incredible if they did not follow the dictates of duty and strategy and secure the stone.

Edward left Dunbar on 2 May with all of Scotland like an open door before him. However, due to a long detour which took him as far as Liddesdale, it was over a month before he reached Edinburgh. During this time, three things must have been obvious to the Comyns: that the Scottish army was scattered and would not reassemble, that Edinburgh Castle would not hold Edward up for long and that short of a totally unforeseen crisis erupting elsewhere he would go at least as far north as Scone, the traditional capital of the kingdom.

Assuming a decision was taken to remove the stone, this could have been effected at any time between the king's departure from Dunbar and his arrival at Perth on 21 June, a period of almost two months. It was not until 10 July that Badenoch and Buchan submitted to him at Montrose.[13]

A question which has exercised various minds at different times is, if the stone was removed, where was it taken to? The romantic view has inclined towards a convenient secret cave – no doubt guarded by withered Celtic bards. Legends have grown up around the evocative local hill of Dunsinane. All this loses validity if we accept that the stone was taken by the Comyns. Their power base was in the north, in a tract of country stretching from Loch Linnhe at the foot of the Great Glen across the roof of Scotland to Buchan Ness.

To remove the stone and simply stick it in a nearby cave, secret or otherwise, would indicate a disregard for security bordering on carelessness. The safest place would be in their own country, Badenoch perhaps rather than Buchan. This was the land of the senior branch of the family and, more importantly, was considerably nearer to hand. The difficulties of transport could have been eased by the rivers Tay and Spey lying alongside much of the route.

Ruthven Castle was demolished in 1718 and a Hanoverian military barracks built on the site.

Possible destinations might have been either Ruthven Castle near Kingussie or the island stronghold of Lochindorb, near Grantown-on-Spey, the two main strongholds from which the Comyns controlled their territory. However, they also had a choice of other castles including Inverlochy, far to the west.

And that is about as exact as we can be. For reasons that will be made clear in the final chapter, it is highly unlikely that knowledge of the original stone's location has survived. All we can say today is that somewhere among the countless stones of Badenoch and Lochaber, there may be one which is rather special.

Lochindorb Castle.

The removal of the original stone must have left the abbot of Scone in a precarious position. Whatever his attitude to it being carried away, without it Thomas can only have looked on the imminent arrival of the king of England with something approaching holy dread. He would have expected Edward to want the stone. Within two days of his arrival in Scotland the king had laid his hands on a large part of what was known as the Treasury of Edinburgh, together with certain items from Holyrood Abbey. These had previously been removed to Berwick, under Edward's influence, in 1291.[14]

Thus, when Edward took the town five years later a fair amount of the loot was conveniently to hand. Among the treasures was the venerated Black Rood of Scotland, a sacred relic brought to the country by St Margaret in the eleventh century. Descriptions vary but it seems to have been a black wooden cross, richly decorated and containing what was believed to be a fragment of the true cross.[15] Edward took this into his possession and carried it round Scotland with him that year. It presumably made a nice pair with the Cross of Neith, of similar sanctity, which he had previously taken from the Welsh.

The rest of the treasure was carefully itemised and packed off to London. By the time Edward had passed through Edinburgh, the stone remained as the only significant item in Scotland which he had not managed to get his hands on. We can assume that Thomas of Scone, as one of the leading churchmen of the country, and a man well-versed in the political situation, was aware of this, together with the much more compelling fact that Edward was moving north in considerable strength.[16]

It is not being suggested here that the abbot tried to palm off a sandstone block in place of the original stone with a sort of blasé impunity. Edward Plantagenet was not the sort of man to appreciate such levity. Another churchman, the dean of St Paul's, had died of heart failure as the result of just a tongue-lashing from the king, and he could easily do things to the abbot of Scone which would have been quite out of place in London.[17] It is more likely that in a desperate situation Thomas resorted to the only plan which might offer him a chance of survival.

Undoubtedly, he would have preferred to hand over something more resembling an enthronement stone. However, we are not talking here of a carefully thought-out plan but rather of a series of hasty improvisations, both on the part of the Comyns and of the abbot left with the task of covering their tracks. If either party had waited till Edward left Stirling, till the undesirable became unavoidable, there would have been less than 48 hours for the task to be accomplished.

Rather than leading a party of monks down to the Annaty Burn to hack out a new stone – though there is a local story to this effect – Thomas might have fallen back on an available substitute, this being a reliquary cover near the altar. As said above, it was worn with use, possibly fitted with rings to make it stand out from all the other stones of Scone Abbey, and sanctified by its association with whatever relic or relics lay beneath. If placed appropriately and decorated with appropriate vestments, it might just have served.

Endnotes

1 Barbour, *The Bruce*, p334.
2 Barrow, *Robert Bruce*, pp95–96.
3 '*Ne avons nous autre chose 'a faire, que 'a vous reaumys gagner?*' D E R Watt et al (eds), *Scotichronicon by Walter Bower* (Aberdeen University Press, 9 volumes, 1987–1999), 2:166.
4 Barrow, *Robert Bruce*, pp83–84.
5 Thomson and Innes, *The Acts of the Parliament of Scotland*, 1:451-3.
6 Skene, *John of Fordun's Chronicle of the Scottish Nation*, pp289–90; Barrow, *Robert Bruce*, p66.
7 Enthronement stones and their function are discussed in Skene, *Coronation Stone*; Stanley, *Westminster Abbey*, pp60–62; F W L Thomas, 'Dunadd, Glassary, Argyllshire; the place of inauguration of the Dalriadic kings', *Proceedings of the Society of Antiquaries of Scotland*, 13 (1879); Welander, *The Stone of Destiny*; P Stanley, *Historical Memorials of Westminster Abbey*.
8 D Macpherson et al (eds), *Rotuli Scotiae in Turri Londinensi et in Domo Capitulari Westmonasteriensi Asservati* (London: Public Record Office, 1814-1819) 1:12a. This also appears in Rhymer, *Foedera, Conventiones, Litterae*, 1:2, p785.
9 G W S Barrow, 'Observations on the Coronation Stone of Scotland', *Scottish Historical Review*, 76 (1997), p119.
10 Skene, *John of Fordun's Chronicle of the Scottish Nation*, p289.
11 Barrow, 'Observations on the Coronation Stone of Scotland', p117.
12 Michael Penman, *Robert the Bruce: King of Scots*, (New Haven & London: Yale University Press, 2014), p95.
13 Bain, *Calendar of Documents*, 2:823.
14 Watson, 'The Black Rood of Scotland', pp37–40. Watson's contention is that the whole of the Scottish treasury was moved to Berwick. This seems to conflict with various English documents, which state that a considerable quantity of valuables, including the crown, orb and sceptre, were found in Edinburgh Castle. The issue is complex and, as far as this book is concerned, peripheral. The main point is that, in his progress through Scotland, Edward was content to take everything that wasn't nailed down. See Stevenson, *Documents Illustrative of the History of Scotland*, 2:415; Hunter, 'King Edward's Spoliations', pp247–49.

15 Watson, 'The Black Rood of Scotland', p30, n1.

16 He was appointed auditor for John Balliol in June 1291. See Francis Palgrave (ed), *Documents and Records illustrating the History of Scotland*, (London: Public Record Office, 1837), Illustrations, 2:3 and 4). He may not actually have acted as an auditor the following year since his name does not appear in the list in Rishanger of those present. Riley, *Willelmi Rishanger*, pp262–65. However, we can take it that he had some involvement in the major issues of the time.

17 Thomas Frederick Tout, *Edward I* (London: Macmillan, 1893), p184.

THE KNOWLEDGE

ISOLATING THE COMYNS as being responsible for removing the original stone provides an explanation for why it was never recovered and why all knowledge of its whereabouts seems to have disappeared. It also explains why Robert the Bruce was unable to arrange for its return to Scone for his coronation of 1306, for the Comyns and Bruce were never reconciled. The last thing they could have been expected to do was hand over the stone to him. Nor could there have been any peacemaking between later generations. It is a rather curious fact that Robert the Bruce outlived not only the two Comyns in question but all their male descendants as well.

Throughout the fairly short remainder of Badenoch's life, he seems to have acted in quite close association with Buchan. After coming into King Edward's peace, they were both sent into England and required to stay south of the Trent.[1] Edward found a use for them the following year when revolt broke out in two separate areas.

In May, William Wallace killed the English sheriff of Lanark. This became the signal for a general uprising in southern and central Scotland. At about the same time, Andrew Murray led the people of Inverness in an assault on Urquhart Castle. Over the course of the summer, the insurgents took one castle after another and gradually cleared the English out of the country north of the Dee.

In June, the two Comyns were sent home by Edward to quell the rising. They seem to have been less than dedicated to their task.[2] Cressingham, the king's treasurer in Scotland, wrote to Edward from Berwick in August saying that the situation north of the Forth was obscure because of the actions of the earls there.[3]

After this, the elder John Comyn of Badenoch seems to fade from the scene. He may have been present at the Battle of Falkirk in 1298.[4] He died around four years later. It was his son, John Comyn the younger, who negotiated the Scottish submission.[5]

However, we can probably assume that whatever the father knew was passed on to his son who, had he not be taken prisoner at Dunbar would most likely have been involved from the beginning.

This younger Comyn of Badenoch seems to have been equally close to the earl of Buchan. The two were together at the council held at Peebles in 1299 when at one point Badenoch became sufficiently enraged as to seize Robert the Bruce by the throat. The following year Badenoch and Buchan commanded two of the three Scottish cavalry brigades that were scattered at the Battle of the Cree. Just prior to this they had represented the Scottish side at the unsuccessful negotiations with Edward at Kirkcudbright.[6]

There is no evidence to suggest that the two were anything other than close allies and quite likely good friends. If, by some accident, the elder Badenoch had neglected to pass on information pertaining to the whereabouts of a certain piece of masonry, we can be reasonably sure that Buchan would have remedied the situation.

Whether the younger Badenoch got round to telling his own son is less certain. Few men can have less foreknowledge of their own deaths than he had. On 10 February 1306 he met with Robert the Bruce in the Greyfriars' church in Dumfries. The subject under discussion was revolution.

For two years, since the general capitulation of 1304, Scotland had scarcely stirred. Now, with Edward ill and obviously nearing the end of his life, the time seemed to be growing ripe for an upheaval. Bruce, having come into the king's peace a clear two years before, was presumably nursing his old aspirations towards kingship. However, as G W S Barrow points out, 'The success of any revolution would depend on the full support or else the elimination of John Comyn of Badenoch'.[7]

Comyn was eliminated. Before the discussion ended, Bruce's dagger had torn a hole in his body and his companions finished off the job. Comyn died suddenly in a place where a man of his time would have felt secure. It is quite possible that any knowledge he may have had went to the grave with him.

If it did not, the line of descent becomes increasingly tenuous after this. John Comyn the younger of Badenoch also had one son, also called John. He was around twelve years old when his father was murdered. He was sent to England after the death and grew up there. He died at Bannockburn. He was fighting on the English side and fell in that first charge of 24 June when Gloucester's heavy cavalry were stopped by the levelled spears of Edward Bruce's division.[8]

This John also left a son, although the tradition was broken by naming him Aymer, presumably after his great-uncle Aymer de Valence. The boy died in childhood, at some time before November 1316; the Badenoch male line was extinct.[9]

The Buchan line had ended even earlier. In 1308 John Comyn of Buchan was defeated by Bruce at Inverurie and afterwards Bruce destroyed his lands and his people. This was the final act in the long struggle between the two factions and special attention was given to ensuring no Comyn supporters remained alive to continue the fight.

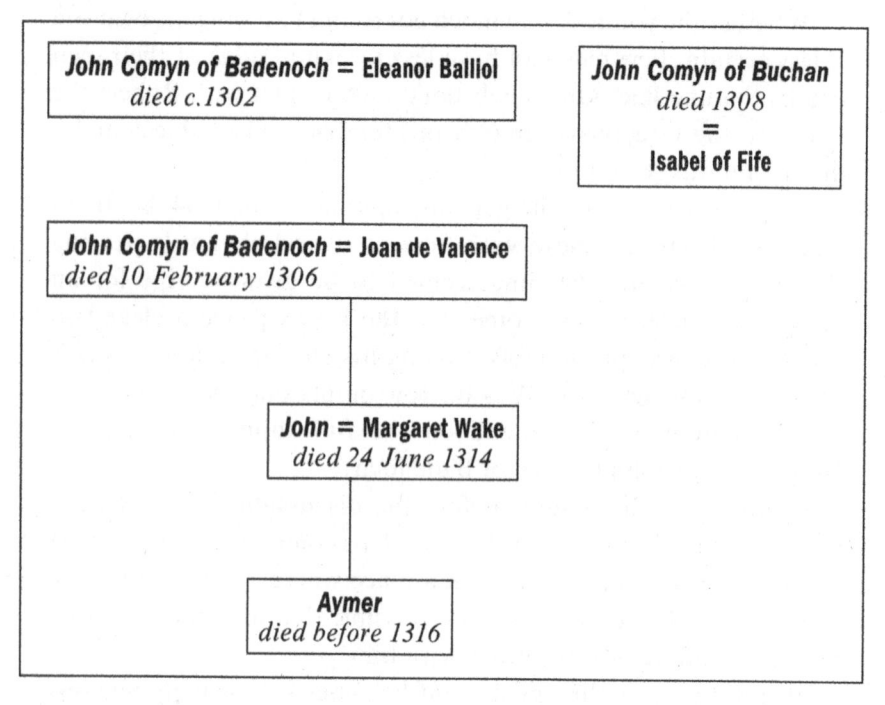

```
John Comyn of Badenoch = Eleanor Balliol      John Comyn of Buchan
died c.1302                                   died 1308
                                              =
                                              Isabel of Fife

John Comyn of Badenoch = Joan de Valence
died 10 February 1306

        John = Margaret Wake
        died 24 June 1314

                Aymer
                died before 1316
```

In an age inured to sack and slaughter, a name was coined to set what Bruce did to the Comyn lands above all the rest – the *heirschip*, or harrying, of Buchan. John Barbour, who came from the northeast, said that the king:

> '... gert his men burn all Bouchane
> Fra end till end, and sparit nane
> And heryit thame on sic maneir
> That eftir that, weile fifty yheir
> Men menyt "the heirschip of Bouchane."'[10]

The earl fled south, to die towards the end of that year. There was little to console him. His land was destroyed, his people slaughtered. He had even lost his wife, for he was married to that Isabel of Fife who, two years before, had galloped off to Bruce's coronation at Scone. English accounts say she was Bruce's lover. If true, this may help to explain the lack of heirs, for Buchan left no legitimate offspring.[11]

Within twenty years of Edward's first invasion of Scotland the two names of Comyn of Badenoch and Comyn of Buchan had withered away. If the stone was moved northwards, some of their people must have been involved. However, even if they survived the ensuing eight years of war against the English and Bruce's slaughter of the Comyns and their supporters in 1308, there would have been no reason to say anything. Bruce was king and remained so. The Comyn cause was lost and with it, we might presume, the knowledge of the last resting place of the original Stone of Destiny.

Endnotes

1 Rothwell, *Walter of Guisborough*, p284. Buchan was not actually named but can be taken as one of the other magnates indicated. He travelled north with Badenoch the following year. See also Bain, *Calendar of Documents*, 2:839.

2 Rothwell, *Walter of Guisborough*, p297; Hog, *Annales sex regum Angliae*, p356.

3 'Sire, la pees dela la meer d'Escoce se tent en coverte, sicom lem dit, parmy le fet dez countes qe la sount' Stevenson, *Documents Illustrative of the History of Scotland*, 2:467.

4 Riley, *Willelmi Rishanger*, p414.

5 F Palgrave (ed), *Documents and Records illustrating the History of Scotland* (London, 1837), 1:129–32.

6 Barrow, *Robert Bruce*, pp140–1, 148.

7 Barrow, *Robert Bruce*, p188.

8 Maxwell, *Chronicle of Lanercost*, p208; Barrow, *Robert Bruce*, pp295–96.

9 Paul, *The Scots Peerage*, 1:509–10.

10 Barbour, *The Bruce*, pp332–34.

11 Paul, *The Scots Peerage*, 2:256–58.

OTHER TITLES FROM TIPPERMUIR BOOKS

Spanish Thermopylae (2009)

Battleground Perthshire (2009)

Perth: Street by Street (2012)

Born in Perthshire (2012)

In Spain with Orwell (2013)

Trust (2014)

Perth: As Others Saw Us (2014)

Love All (2015)

A Chocolate Soldier (2016)

The Early Photographers of Perthshire (2016)

Taking Detective Novels Seriously: The Collected Crime Reviews of Dorothy L Sayers (2017)

Walking with Ghosts (2017)

No Fair City: Dark Tales from Perth's Past (2017)

The Tale o the Wee Mowdie that wantit tae ken wha keeched on his heid (2017)

Hunters: Wee Stories from the Crescent: A Reminiscence of Perth's Hunter Crescent (2017)

A Little Book of Carol's (2018)

Flipstones (2018)

Perth: Scott's Fair City: The Fair Maid of Perth & Sir Walter Scott – A Celebration & Guided Tour (2018)

God, Hitler, and Lord Peter Wimsey: Selected Essays, Speeches and Articles by Dorothy L Sayers (2019)

Perth & Kinross: A Pocket Miscellany: A Companion for Visitors and Residents (2019)

The Piper of Tobruk: Pipe Major Robert Roy, MBE, DCM (2019)

The 'Gig Docter o Athole': Dr William Irvine & The Irvine Memorial Hospital (2019)

Afore the Highlands: The Jacobites in Perth, 1715–16 (2019)

'Where Sky and Summit Meet': Flight Over Perthshire – A History: Tales of Pilots, Airfields, Aeronautical Feats, & War (2019)

Diverted Traffic (2020)

Authentic Democracy: An Ethical Justification of Anarchism (2020)

'If Rivers Could Sing': A Scottish River Wildlife Journey. A Year in the Life of the River Devon as it flows through the Counties of Perthshire, Kinross-shire & Clackmannanshire (2020)

A Squatter o Bairnrhymes (2020)

In a Sma Room Songbook: From the Poems by William Soutar (2020)

The Nicht Afore Christmas: the much-loved yuletide tale in Scots (2020)

Ice Cold Blood (2021)

The Perth Riverside Nursery & Beyond: A Spirit of Enterprise and Improvement (2021)

Fatal Duty: The Scottish Police Force to 1952: Cop Killers, Killer Cops & More (2021)

The Shanter Legacy: The Search for the Grey Mare's Tail (2021)

'Dying to Live': The Story of Grant McIntyre, Covid's Sickest Patient (2021)

The Black Watch and the Great War (2021)

Beyond the Swelkie: A Collection of Poems & Writings to Mark the Centenary of George Mackay Brown (2021)

Sweet F.A. (2022)

A War of Two Halves (2022)

A Scottish Wildlife Odyssey (2022)

In the Shadow of Piper Alpha (2022)

Mind the Links: Golf Memories (2022)

Perthshire 101: A Poetic Gazetteer of the Big County (2022)

The Banes o the Turas: An Owersettin in Scots o the Poems bi Pino Mereu scrievit in Tribute tae Hamish Henderson (2022)

Walking the Antonine Wall: A Journey from East to West Scotland (2022)

The Japan Lights: On the Trail of the Scot Who Lit Up Japan's Coast (2023)

Fat Girl Best Friend: 'Claiming Our Space' – Plus Size Women in Film & Television (2023)

Wild Quest Britain: A Nature Journey of Discovery through England, Scotland & Wales – from Lizard Point to Dunnet Head (2023)

Guid Mornin! Guid Nicht! (2023)

Madainn Mhath! Oidhche Mhath! (2023)

Who's Aldo? (2023)

A History of Irish Republicanism in Dundee (c1840 to 1985) (Rùt Nic Foirbeis, 2024)

The Stone of Destiny & The Scots (John Hulbert, 2024)

FORTHCOMING

William Soutar: Complete Poetry, Volumes I & II (Published Work) (Paul S Philippou (Editor-in-Chief) & Kirsteen McCue and Philippa Osmond-Williams (editors), 2024)

William Soutar: Complete Poetry, Volume III (Miscellaneous & Unpublished Poetry) (Paul S Philippou (Editor-in-Chief) & Kirsteen McCue and Philippa Osmond-Williams (editors), 2025)

William Soutar: Complete Poetry, Volume IV (Prose Selections) (Paul S Philippou (Editor-in-Chief) & Kirsteen McCue and Philippa Osmond-Williams (editors), 2026)

The Whole Damn Town (Hannah Ballantyne, 2024)

Balkan Rhapsody (Maria Kassimova-Moisset, translated by Iliyana Nedkova Byrne, 2024)

The Black Watch From the Crimean War to the Second Boer War (Derek Patrick and Fraser Brown, 2024)

Salvage (Mark Baillie, 2024).

TIPPERMUIR
· BOOKS LIMITED ·

All Tippermuir Books titles are available from bookshops and online booksellers. They can also be purchased directly (with free postage & packing (UK only) – minimum charges for overseas delivery) from **www.tippermuirbooks.co.uk**